Private Prisons in America

A CRITICAL RACE PERSPECTIVE

Michael A. Hallett

UNIVERSITY OF ILLINOIS PRESS

URBANA AND CHICAGO

Library of Congress Cataloging-in-Publication Data
Hallett, Michael A.
Private prisons in America : a critical race perspective /
Michael A. Hallett.
p.   cm. — (Critical perspectives in criminology)
Includes bibliographical references and index.
ISBN-13: 978-0-252-03069-7 (cloth : alk. paper)
ISBN-10: 0-252-03069-9 (cloth : alk. paper)
ISBN-13: 978-0-252-07308-3 (pbk. : alk. paper)
ISBN-10: 0-252-07308-8 (pbk. : alk. paper)
1. Corrections—Contracting out—United States.
2. Discrimination in criminal justice administration—
United States. I. Title. II. Series.
HV9469.H256   2006
365'.973—dc22   2005017072

This book is dedicated to Hal Pepinsky, professor of criminal justice at Indiana University, Bloomington. I have been privileged to study and visit with Hal on many occasions, first as a student and later as a colleague. These visits are always lengthy conversations about peace, about real "social security," and about maintaining a healthy skepticism for legally imposed "order." Professor Pepinsky helped me to see punishment as something far more complex and deeply revealing than simple agendas for "crime control" imply. I must go further, however, and offer my thanks to Hal for what I know to be his personal commitment to students, of which I am one of many. More than any single person, Hal helped me to see that imprisonment in the Anglo world—rather than being a force for justice—is today a mechanism for injustice and social stratification as powerful as any undemocratic state. America's despotic lust for punishing and exploiting those who are different is rooted in our patriarchic and colonial past, as noted even by Alexis de Tocqueville. The practice of American imprisonment has long been a mechanism of social control that merely perpetuates and deepens the preexisting imbalances of power endured by those most often imprisoned. The power-laden social theater of imprisonment continues unabated today, only now (once again) for private profit.

CONTENTS

FOREWORD

RANDALL G. SHELDEN

During the past two decades American
society has experienced a growing crisis in
the way it responds to crime. On the one
hand, if you compare the crime rate in 1971
with what it was thirty years later, you will
find it is essentially the same. Yet incarceration rates have zoomed upward by almost
500 percent during this time, caused
mostly by the "war on drugs" that has systematically targeted racial minorities and
the poor—especially African Americans.
The incarceration rate for African
Americans is around eight times greater
than for whites, whereas a black child has
a one in four chance of ending up in prison.
White prisoners are now in the numerical
minority within the prison system. Urban
communities have been devastated by this
imprisonment binge. Meanwhile, mass
imprisonment is good for many businesses
and the growing "crime-control industry."
Clearly, something is amiss in this country.

Michael Hallett's book gets to the heart
of the matter. Hallett appears to be a sort
of reincarnation of some of the notables of
what used to be called "penology," namely,

people like Thorsten Sellin, Howard Becker, Georg Rusche, and Otto Kirchheimer. All of these men used classic sociological analysis in their examination of the modern system of punishment. The book you have before you is one of the few in the current era (aside from of a few notable exceptions, such as David Garland) to extend this kind of analysis. The recent trend toward greater and greater reliance on incarceration as a tool for "social control"—more specifically, as a method of controlling the "surplus population" or "dangerous classes"—forces us to look beyond the trees and examine the forest. In Hallett's book we get a rare glimpse into the past and its link to the present and the future. This link, I believe, is the intersection of two crucial sociological variables: race and the profit motive of capitalism.

Toward the end of Chapter 3 Hallett provides a succinct summary of the major thesis of his book when he writes: "Private prisons reveal truths about our culture and social system that have little to do with crime control, but have much to do, instead, with the often racist and exploitative character of our capitalistic economic system." Paraphrasing the excellent work of Katherine Beckett, Hallett, again in this same chapter, notes how the perception of poverty has shifted from the "deserving" poor of rural whites during the Great Depression to the "undeserving" poor of urban blacks. From this perspective, incarceration has little to do with crime per se—and especially has little to do with reducing crime and suffering among our citizens. We lock people up not to reduce crime and protect victims, but to help control a growing surplus population, while simultaneously supporting private interests, such as profits for capitalists and votes for "law and order" politicians.

Hallett explores, in Chapter 2 (one of the best histories of punishment and imprisonment I have ever read), the rise of the "Convict Lease" system in the southern states after the close of the Civil War. This was, as all previous research has proven, an attempt both to control the former black slaves (and, in fact, perpetuate other forms of slavery) and to aid capitalist profit seeking. It is at this time that we find a correlation with the rise in the black incarceration rate (booming upward throughout the South, bypassing in both numbers and rates those for whites) and the early beginnings of prison privatization. Then, about one hundred years later, we find a dramatic increase in black incarceration rates—fueled by the "war on drugs"—along with, once again, the emergence of prison privatization, led by two corporations, Corrections Corporation of America and Wackenhut Corrections Corporation. As Hallett notes at the end of the book: "The racial characteristics of modern private prisons cannot be ignored for what they still represent: a racialized, coercive, for-profit imprisonment practice disproportionately utilizing young black men for its system of economic production."

Hallett's critical analysis—too often missing in current criminological research (which too often benefits from corporate or governmental handouts, or both, for "correct" research topics) —looks even further and finds the timing of the recent incarceration binge with privatization corresponds precisely with the rise of a conservative domination of all governmental functions. This includes, very importantly, the emphasis (pushed with almost equal force by both Republicans and Democrats) on reducing the role played by the government (especially when it comes to traditional forms of welfare). "Get the government off our backs" is the rallying cry from conservatives and growing numbers of "liberals." What these groups fail to add is "unless it benefits big business" ("corporate welfare," and so on). Thus, it is not too surprising to find that since the early 1980s the distribution of wealth has been skewed ever more toward the richest proportion of the population, so that by the end of the 1990s the top 1 percent of wealth holders had about 48 percent of all financial wealth and the next 19 percent had just about all the rest, with the remaining 80 percent of the population holding onto less than 5 percent.

Hallett provides a unique look at one manifestation of this "less government" movement, with a critical analysis of so-called faith-based correctional programming. It is through this kind of analysis that we get an even deeper insight into what the conservative crime-control policies are all about. It is here that we see the movement away from understanding the quite obvious and well-documented (with more than one hundred years of research, especially the "social disorganization" perspective, which Hallett discusses at length in Chapter 4) social sources of crime (poverty and social inequality) to seeing crime as a "moral and ethical" problem. It reminds me of the old criminal-as-sinner perspective, which led to the so-called Pennsylvania Plan (not coincidentally, we find this model of prison alive and well in our growing "supermax" prisons with twenty-four-hour solitary confinement and "warehousing" of prisoners). Thus, the offender is not a product of his or her environment, but is rather some "evil" or "ungodly" or "immoral" person. Hallett's analysis of the rise of this "faith-based" movement utilizes some of the now classic works of Joseph Gusfield and Howard Becker by focusing on "moral entrepreneurs" and "symbolic crusades." It has been a long time since anyone has done this and resurrected this method of analysis (those of us who began their criminological careers in the 1960s and 1970s remember this kind of research), and Hallett's chapter on this subject provides some important insights.

In his concluding chapter, Hallett brings his analysis to a critical juncture, namely, the fact that recent trends in "crime control" do not come close to effectively reducing crime, since maintaining a steady supply of criminals (even if they have to be invented, as through the drug war, for instance) is very profitable for those who benefit from the "crime-control industry." In short, as one of Hallett's chapter subheadings reads, we have "social disorganization as market opportunity." Large numbers of disfranchised, dispossessed, urban minorities, reduced to what Marx once called the "surplus population," are now viewed, like the slaves of the nineteenth-century South, as valuable "commodities" for not just those who operate private prisons but also literally hundreds of businesses, large and small, who are the much sought-after "vendors" of the criminal justice industrial complex, not to mention the abundant and almost unlimited supply of career opportunities for thousands of job seekers, especially college graduates from "criminal justice" programs. Crime control, in short, is big business, and Michael Hallett's book provides a deeper understanding of what we all face, both today and in the future.

ACKNOWLEDGMENTS

In May 1997, I became an "activist" associated with a state employees' labor union, the Tennessee State Employees' Association (TSEA), to help fend off a take-over bid by Corrections Corporation of America (CCA) for the entire Tennessee prison system. CCA had tried in the past to secure a ninety-nine-year lease on Tennessee's inmates, and state employee and prisoners' rights activists in the state were determined to fight. I ended up testifying, along with many others, before the Tennessee legislature's Select Oversight Committee on Corrections (SOCC) as an expert witness against the proposal, educating myself on many of the micromanagement issues associated with prison privatization presented in Chapter 6. Since that time, I have continued my research, testified in front of other legislatures on issues related to the topic, volunteered as a consultant to activist groups fighting private prisons around the country, and helped construct journalistic stories on private prisons appearing in the *Nation, Mother Jones,* and *Business Week.* Along the way,

I have encountered many souls on both sides of the issue who have helped shape my thinking.

First and foremost, I wish to thank Robert Coles, whose early work *Children of Crisis* and recent surprising correspondence with me helped steel my determination to see this project through. Like his frequent protagonists, Dorothy Day and Peter Maurin, Professor Coles's persistent theme in psychiatric biography—*that we must be caretakers of others in order to find our own path*—lies at the core of this project for me. I cannot fathom how it is that we undertake an agenda for profitability through imprisonment of human beings and come away with anything approximating democracy. To me, the story of for-profit imprisonment is a story about the world on fire.

Staughton and Alice Lynd, two longtime activists, invited me to Youngstown, Ohio, to visit with their group, the Prison Forum, in 1999. My visit with them in particular exposed me to the racial claims being made by CCA at the time (that CCA was good for the black community and provided good jobs for minorities at its Youngstown, Ohio, facility— in a for-profit prison that held 86 percent black males) and helped me realize some things about the racial dynamics of private prisons I was not yet prepared to see. My former boss Dr. Frank Lee encouraged and helped me in early research, and his quiet southern skepticism about privatization continues to be instructive. Charles Thomas, who will probably not recall our meeting in Oklahoma City where we sat on a panel together, served as an early foil for my inclinations regarding prison privatization and remains a key resource to the privatization research community. Eric Bates, Barry Yoemann, and Ashley Hunt are three journalists who have shared in the journey. David Shichor and Mike Gilbert provided much help on earlier work. Professor David Simon read portions of this work, as did James Austin, whose work I have used so much of in the classroom myself. Dr. Scott Camp, of the Federal Bureau of Prisons, reviewed my work and provided early support. As an author of the Abt Associates report on private prisons and other work, Dr. Camp's knowledge and collegiality have been inspiring to me. The work and endorsement of Professor Malcolm Feeley mean more to me than I can say.

Randall Shelden's work and critical support on this project have been pillars of this undertaking from the beginning, since I have drawn upon his "critical" perspective for years in the classroom and in my own thinking. Professor Michael Welch, with whom I got acquainted late in this project, has produced literally voluminous work on corrections and privatization. His prolific recent work is like a nighttime bolt of lightning, revealing new terrain. This project greatly benefited from Professor Welch's constructive review. Todd Clear offered a supportive critique. As will become apparent, the prolific writings of Cornel West have had a profound influence. From his writings and extracurricular work I can see that he is a great teacher, in the best sense of the word. Though I have never met him, I would also like to thank David Garland, whose exquisite writings on punishment have been inspirational. Three former professors, Michael Musheno and Dennis Palumbo at Arizona State University and Marty Schwartz at Ohio University, laid "critical" foundations for my thinking. My editor at the University of Illinois Press, Kerry Callahan, has been totally supportive and extremely professional, a true intellectual, and a total pleasure to work with. Thanks to Annette Wenda for her meticulous copyediting work. My wife, Karin Hallett, helped in innumerable ways, both academic and otherwise. Finally, this book is dedicated to Hal Pepinsky, professor of criminal justice at Indiana University, Bloomington.

ONE

Race, Crime, and For-Profit Imprisonment

Imagine what the results would be if the impact of mass incarceration on whites was comparable to its effects on blacks. If nearly 10 percent of all white people were placed under correctional control tomorrow, would there be a national outcry? Of course there would. But today's penal policies are not likely to produce this kind of non-racialized police state. Their character is instead to be found in America's intertwined histories of prisons, penal reform, and racism.

—Alex Lichtenstein, "The Private and the Public in Penal History"

It is perhaps astonishing to realize that the Thirteenth Amendment to the U.S. Constitution—widely known for "abolishing" slavery—also authorized the "involuntary servitude" of prisoners as a punishment for crime: "Neither slavery nor involuntary servitude, except as a punishment for crime whereof the party shall have been duly convicted, shall exist within the United States, or any place subject to their jurisdiction." During the operation of the U.S. "Convict Lease" system from 1865 to the 1920s, the Thirteenth Amendment simultaneously enabled the continuation of racialized forced labor in the South at what was supposed to be the start of freedom for African American slaves. Upon release from their former owners' captivity, "emancipated" slaves often had nowhere to go—and found themselves designated "trespassers," "disturbers of the peace," "vagrants," or "loiterers" on their former owners' plantations (Shelden, 2001, p. 170). With white southern elites caught between the legal restrictions of abolition and the paramount need for cheap labor, Convict Leasing emerged as a uniquely southern solution for solving the postbellum labor shortage—and a powerful vehicle for the continuation of white supremacy. As W. E. B. Du Bois noted more than a century ago about Convict Leasing: "The South believed in slave labor, and was thoroughly convinced that free Negroes would not work steadily or effectively. The whites were determined after the war, therefore, to restore slavery in everything but name" (2002, p. 84).

Once imprisoned for petty crimes, former slaves, now inmates, were leased in large numbers to private vendors as a source of forced labor, to become the foundation of lucrative, profit-driven, white-owned businesses (Lichtenstein, 1996; Curtin, 2000; Mancini, 1996). As Randall Shelden writes about the Convict Lease system immediately after the Civil War, "One result of this practice was the shift in prison populations to predominantly African-American" (2001, p. 170). Shelden's data from Tennessee's Main Prison at Nashville indicate that blacks sent to prison increased dramatically after the Civil War, whereas the proportion of whites sent to prison decreased (see Table 1.1). After an initial service fee to the state for "lease" of the convicts, private vendors merely housed and fed laborers in their charge. Early industries utilizing convict labor included coal mining, logging, turpentine production, railroad construction, and farmwork (Mancini, 1996).

Developed in the context of the abolition of slavery, the Convict Lease system engendered a racialized but legal form of coercive labor practice, criminalizing the activities of newly freed slaves for being vagrants

Table 1.1 Civil War–era Incarceration Rates by Race

Date	Total	White	Black	Percent Black
Oct. 1855	200	134	66	33.0
Nov. 1867	485	202	283	58.3
Oct. 1869	551	198	353	64.0

Source: Sheldon 2001, p 171.

or paupers or migrants and sending them in large numbers to prison (Lichtenstein, 1996). As such, the Convict Lease system kept alive a racially disproportionate system of involuntary servitude—*and a slavery-era understanding of captives as legally exploitable commodities.* Not until organized free labor gained voice enough to remove rival convict laborers from the marketplace, in the early 1900s, was the Convict Lease system transformed into the strictly public works "chain gang" road crews of the "New South" (Oshinsky, 1996; Mancini, 1978, 1996; Hallett, 1996).

This book examines the reappearance of for-profit imprisonment in the United States and focuses specifically on the racial history of imprisonment for private profit. Although other forms of mercantile enterprise with prisoners existed prior to the Convict Lease system—for example, inmate labor contracts inside penitentiaries and short-term leasing of prisoners for work outside the prison—these arrangements were generally undertaken "with the expectation that the state would share in any surpluses" and were driven largely by prison administrators seeking to reduce costs (Feeley, 2002, p. 333). Modern private prison systems, like the Convict Lease system, however, reap profits for private owners and shareholders.

Prior to the Revolutionary War, private profit was also made by British, British colonial, Dutch, and other merchant shippers through the practice of transporting criminals, debtors, and eventually free indentured servants to the colonies for work on plantations. After the Revolution, the practice of transportation was stopped, however, exacerbating the colonies' reliance on slavery (Smith, 1965). After the Civil War, the Convict Lease system again reinscribed forced labor as a viable source of economic production. As W. E. B. Du Bois argued in 1901: "The Convict Lease system is the slavery in private hands of persons convicted of crimes and misdemeanors in the courts" (2002, p. 83).

The most striking thing about the reemergence of for-profit imprisonment in the United States, however, is not simply that it has reappeared, but that it should once again involve the disproportionate captivity of black men. During the two periods of U.S. history in which corrections policy facilitated private profit through imprisonment, first during the proprietary operation of the Convict Lease system and again today (since the mid-1980s), the incarceration of disproportionate numbers of African American males has been the industry's chief source of revenue. Although the nature of prisoners' commodity value has changed somewhat in modern times—prisoners are no longer profitable solely for their labor, but for their bodily ability to generate per diem payments for their private keepers—imprisonment for private profit is once again a viable economic industry in the United States.

According to the most recent data, 66 percent of inmates currently held in private prisons are racial minorities, with African Americans constituting the single largest group (43.9 percent) (Austin & Coventry, 2001, p. 41).[1] For-profit prisons are predominantly located in the American South, with western private prison facilities in Texas constituting the single largest rival to southern dominance in this area (see Figure 1.6 below). It is only since the 1980s, however, that blacks began again to dominate U.S. prison populations, as the drug war reached full implementation (Wacquant, 1999, p. 215)—and only then that for-profit prisons reappeared. As discussed in more detail below, the incarceration rate for African American males in the United States is currently more than eight times that of white males and is largely a result of convictions for nonviolent drug and property offenders.

Race, Crime and Mass Imprisonment: Private Prisons Again in America?

As documented by Thorsten Sellin (1976), slavery and punishment have coexisted throughout history, in places as disparate as ancient Greece and Rome to nineteenth-century Russia and the United States. That the American Thirteenth Amendment simultaneously abolished slavery and initiated "involuntary servitude" in the United States speaks to the duality of slavery and punishment in the American context. As noted above, the Convict Lease system was wielded almost exclusively against people of African descent and was never extensively developed in the North (Colvin, 1997; Lichtenstein, 1996; Curtin, 2000; Ayers, 1984).

When certain segments of the population become the focus of such disproportionately high rates of imprisonment that incarceration becomes a common characteristic of their experience as a social group, David Garland suggests that a social phenomenon of "mass imprisonment" has emerged (2001b). Garland argues that "imprisonment becomes mass imprisonment when it ceases to be the incarceration of individual offenders and becomes the systematic imprisonment of whole groups of the population. [When] . . . imprisonment ceases to be the fate of a few criminal individuals, and becomes a shaping institution for whole sectors of the population," more than just "crime control" is understood to be taking place (p. 2). In the midst of today's *second* era of mass incarceration of African American men, produced as a result of the recent "war on drugs," the renewed private commodification of black prisoners becomes all the more troublesome.

Whereas the private prison industry has reemerged today because of contemporary agendas in the U.S. criminal justice system—namely, the war on drugs—it is important to note that this drug war has focused on only a very narrow spectrum of drug use in the American population, specifically drugs used by African American men, namely, crack cocaine. As documented in Chapter 2, the aftermath of the Civil War also produced a period in which the most typical crimes of whites were overlooked while the criminal justice system focused on the most typical crimes of blacks. As contemporary self-report data indicate, for example, there is widespread drug use by white middle-class American teens—yet law enforcement raids by heavily armed SWAT-team drug–task force members storming through college dormitories seem ludicrous (Donziger, 1996, p. 115). As the Justice Policy Institute (2002) recently pointed out, there are far more African American men in prison than are currently attending universities in the United States. This is not to mention the ill effect the drug war has had on the problems of violence and family breakup in minority communities themselves (Rose & Clear, 1998). As Steven Donziger notes in his book *The Real War on Crime: The Report of the National Criminal Justice Commission:*

> Given its impact on minorities, the drug war is a classic case where the treatment for the problem might be worse than the disease. After police raid a drug corner, drug dealers usually pick up and move their operation to another block to continue. Police could never really *stop* the drug trade, they could only *displace* it. In the process of that displacement, violence erupted as dealers jockeyed to control market share. . . . [T]he amount of trafficking, lawlessness, and violence in the United States increased along with the all-out attempt to capture, prosecute, and imprison traffickers and users of illicit drugs. (1996, p. 119)

Table 1.2 shows the disparities between white and black incarceration rates, particularly during the height of the drug war. As argued in more detail below, *it was the hyperincarceration of black males in the early years of the drug war that resurrected the for-profit imprisonment industry in the 1980s.* The events of September 11, 2001, as will be shown, are also enabling the industry to focus on newer "enemies," namely, illegal immigrants incarcerated through the federal detention process (Wacquant, 1999; see also especially Welch, 2005). In both cases, the imprisonment of darker-skinned "others" is used to sustain, expand, and rhetorically justify the profitable imprisonment of captives. As shown in Table 1.2, the incarceration rate for white males in the United States in 1997 was 990 per 100,000. The incarceration rate for black males in the United States for that same year, however, was 6,838 per 100,000.

That the historical pattern of racially distinct commerce in imprisoned human beings has returned in the United States, and that this commerce has been generated again by a crackdown on predominantly disfranchised minorities, reveals much about the operation and use of punishment in the United States. As the drug war got fully under way through the late 1980s and early 1990s, prisons became overcrowded with predominantly African American men. The disparity first appeared greatest in the South, and Corrections Corporation of America—headquartered in Tennessee—put forward its first contract proposal to capitalize on what became a classic supply-and-demand shortfall in prison space:

Table 1.2 U.S. Incarceration Rates, by Race and Gender, 1985–1997.

	White		Black	
	Male	Female	Male	Female
1985	528	27	3544	183
1986	570	29	3850	189
1987	594	35	3943	216
1988	629	41	4441	257
1989	685	47	5066	321
1990	711	48	5161	329
1991	732	51	5503	346
1992	766	53	5793	356
1993	797	55	6032	393
1994	842	61	6443	426
1995	907	65	6618	456
1996	933	71	6608	472
1997	990	76	6838	491

Number and rate (per 100,000 adult residents in each group) of adults held in state or federal prisons or local jails.

Source: U.S. Department of Justice, Bureau of Justice Statistics, *Correctional Populations in the United States, 1995,* NCJ-163916. Tables 1.6 and 1.7; *1997,* NCJ 177613, Tables 1.6 and 1.7 (Washington, D.C.: U.S. Department of Justice). Table adapted by SOURCEBOOK staff.

high demand for imprisonment with low supply of prison cells. Figure 1.1 shows that by 2003 the incarceration rate was at an all-time high, with racial disparities among white, black, and Hispanic male incarceration rates in the United States profoundly high—and greatest for black males in the prime of life. "Mass imprisonment" indeed.

How can it be that in the United States of America *prison* is the predicted destination for whole classes of people—to the point where imprisonment has, once again, become a for-profit industry? As shown in Figure 1.2, during 2003, for every 100,000 black males in the United States aged twenty to forty four, 36,932 of them were in prison. The numbers per

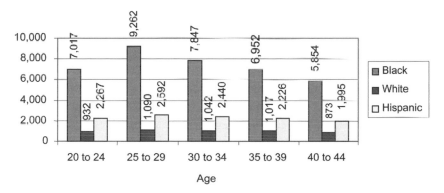

Figure 1.1 2003 incarceration rate per 100,000 U.S. resident males by age and race or ethnicity. Source: U.S. Department of Justice.

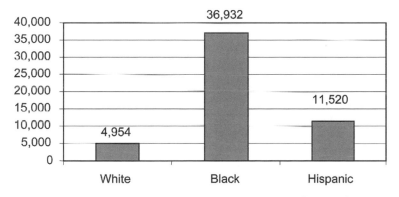

Figure 1.2 2003 incarceration rate per 100,000 U.S. resident males, twenty-two to forty-four years old, by race or ethnicity. Source: U.S. Department of Justice.

100,000 Hispanic and 100,000 white males the same age were 11,520 and 4,954, respectively. As shown in Figure 1.3, black males constitute the smallest numeric grouping of males in the population, whereas their rate of incarceration is nearly eight times higher than that of white males and more than three times higher than that of Hispanic males. Despite being the numeric minority, more black males than either white males or Hispanic males were state or federal prisoners in 2003 (Figure 1.4). A total of 2,085,620 prisoners were held in some form of confinement (state

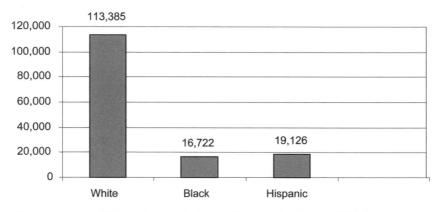

Figure 1.3 2003 U.S. male population in thousands. Source: U.S. Department of Justice.

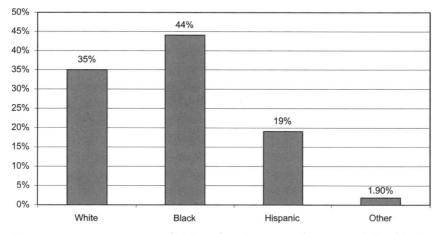

Figure 1.4 2003 percentage of U.S. male prisoners under state or federal jurisdiction. Source: U.S. Department of Justice.

or federal prisons or in local jails) in 2003, which in this context is best viewed as a vast potential market opportunity.

The Argument Presented: A Race and Power Book

This book is about how race and power impact an important facet of the American criminal justice system, the reemergent for-profit imprisonment industry. Our discussion will of necessity examine the historical operation of the Convict Lease system after the Civil War. This is appropriate because the two times in U.S. history when black men have found themselves victims of hyperincarceration, during the operation of the Convict Lease system and again during the more contemporary war on drugs, private entrepreneurs emerged to capitalize on strong public sentiment against a "black crime problem."

The analysis of contemporary for-profit imprisonment offered here suggests private prisons are best understood not as the product of increasing crime rates (rates have been falling for many years), but instead as the latest chapter in a larger historical pattern of oppressive and legal discrimination aimed primarily at African American men. This history reveals a pattern of black offenders in particular being treated very differently than their white counterparts as both groups have coexisted in the matrix of capitalism, criminal justice, and American racial politics. By documenting that policy shifts focused on crimes committed disproportionately by African Americans preceded the rise of for-profit imprisonment both times it has emerged in U.S. history and that imprisonment of African American men has been the mainstay of for-profit imprisonment whenever it has emerged, this book explores how race continues to play a powerful role in the uses and forms of American imprisonment. This imprisonment—rather than being a force for justice—is today a mechanism for injustice and social stratification as powerful as any undemocratic state. As noted even by Alexis de Tocqueville: "While society in the United States gives the example of the most extended liberty, the prisons of the same country offer the spectacle of the most complete despotism" (Beaumont & Tocqueville, 1964, p. 47).

In short, this book offers a less than conventional view of how imprisonment operates in society—a view that questions the instrumentalist "crime control" version of incarceration by documenting historical and present-day discrepancies in the racial composition of inmates made profitable by the for-private-profit imprisonment industry. By showing how imprisonment serves numerous agendas other than crime control, this book also hopes to expand awareness about the expansion of imprisonment in the United States and to foster critical thinking about its use. That the for-profit imprisonment industry has so exclusively relied upon the confinement of minorities throughout its history reveals more about the social context of imprisonment than it does about the crime problem. The history of for-profit imprisonment arguably also reveals more about imprisonment's de facto social purpose: control of those who are different or labeled "dangerous," even for mostly nonviolent crimes.

Messages about punishment carry symbolic import for the social order. According to David Garland: "More than most legal phenomena, the practices of prohibiting and punishing are directed outwards, towards the public—towards 'society'—and claim to embody the sentiments and the moral vision not of lawyers or judges, but of 'the people'" (1991, p. 192).

This work builds upon an established tradition in critical criminology that views American "wars" on crime as focused not on the powerful or wealthy members of the dominant culture, but instead on alien or marginalized segments of the community, branded as symbolic enemies and who are comparatively marginal in the power structure of society (Gusfield, 1963; Tonry, 1995; Reiman, 2004). The American incarceration rate is far higher today than it was in 1980 and far higher than that of any similarly prosperous society in the world. What does this reveal about our society?

What "Other" Agendas?

President Bill Clinton liked to brag about how much he had done for the economy while he was in office. He would repeatedly explain that, according to many indexes, the American economy was at its "strongest ever" near the close of the twentieth century—with the lowest rates of unemployment and inflation in a generation and a tight labor market pushing wages higher. Another less widely cited index, however, clouded this picture of robust societal health (Freeman, 2001, p. 23): the American incarceration rate was at an all-time high, 682 per 100,000 (Bureau of Justice Statistics 1999, p. 497). Clinton, of course, forgot to mention this. Expanded dramatically by the implementation of policies associated with the "war on drugs," incarceration rates skyrocketed in the 1980s and 1990s (Figure 1.5).

Combined with the fact that the highest concentrations of unem-

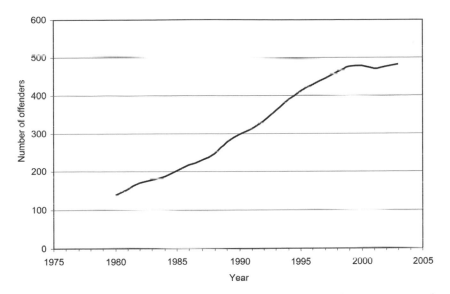

Figure 1.5 U.S. incarceration rate, 1980–2003. Source: U.S. Department of Justice.

ployment in the United States are found among urban African American men, high rates of incarceration and simultaneously low rates of official unemployment are suspicious indeed. These figures raise the possibility that incarceration began to *replace* social welfare as a primary means of coping with joblessness during the 1980s and 1990s, at precisely the time popular support for "welfare reform" reached its zenith (Simon, 1993; Western & Beckett, 1999; Sampson & Wilson, 2000; Wilson, 1996; Mauer, 2000). As Beckett and Sasson point out regarding the supposed "success" of welfare reform as it relates to rising incarceration rates: "Reduced welfare expenditures are not indicative of a shift toward reduced government intervention in social life, but rather a shift toward a more exclusionary and punitive approach to the regulation of social marginality" (2000a, pp. 46–47). The incarceration of young African American men in particular as a social group "has escalated to heights experienced by no other group in history, even under repressive authoritarian regimes and in Soviet-style societies" (Wacquant, 2001, p. 105).

The predominant "targets" of the drug war were without question impoverished urban African American males not active in the formalized workforce (Tonry, 1995; Lauritsen & Sampson, 1998). According to Lauritsen and Sampson:

From 1965 through the early 1980s, blacks were approximately twice as likely as whites to be arrested for a drug-related offense. Following the federal government's initiation of the "war on drugs," black arrest rates skyrocketed, while white arrest rates increased only slightly. By the end of the 1980s, blacks were more than five times more likely than whites to be arrested for drug-related offenses. It is highly unlikely that these race differences are a simple reflection of substance abuse patterns, since drug arrests grew at a time when national self-report data showed that drug use was declining among both blacks and whites. Rather, these differences reflect the government's targeting and enforcement of specific types of drug use and trafficking. (1998, p. 63)

"But It's Only 10 Percent": The Problem with Making For-Profit Prisons Comfortable

A common sentiment among advocates of for-profit imprisonment is that the percentage of inmates housed in private facilities as compared to public facilities today is still "less than 10 percent" of the total inmate population (Austin & Coventry, 2003). Although it is true that only roughly 7 percent of today's prisoners are housed in private prisons—7 percent of today's prison population constitutes 95,522 people.

Private prisons today constitute *the nation's fourth largest prison system*. Whereas the federal prison system has recently surpassed all of the individual states in terms of size, only Texas and California today have higher inmate populations than the American private prison industry. In short, literally *tens of thousands* of people are confined in for-profit prisons in America today, the majority of whom are racial or ethnic minorities confined for low-level nonviolent immigration, property, or drug offenses (Welch, 2005).

According to the U.S. Department of Justice, in September 2001, fourteen private corporations operated prisons with a capacity of roughly 119,000 beds, with private prison operators working in thirty-two U.S. states, Puerto Rico, Iraq, Great Britain, South Africa, New Zealand, and Australia. The U.S. federal government is one of the largest users of for-profit imprisonment, particularly by the newly formed Bureau of Immigration and Customs Enforcement (BICE) (formerly the Immigration and Naturalization Service or INS) and the Federal Bureau of Prisons (BOP). Among federal prisoners, many of those housed in private facilities are non-U.S. citizens incarcerated for immigration violations by the BICE

(Welch, 2005, 2002; James, 2002). Between 1995 and 2000, the number of inmates in for-profit facilities increased by 458.6 percent (Maguire & Pastore, 2002, table 6.0004). In the aftermath of September 11, 2001, the U.S. federal prison system has the fastest-increasing rate of incarceration of any prison system in the country, prompting growing reliance by the U.S. Federal Bureau of Prisons on private prison contracts (Welch, 2004, 2002; James, 2002). Between 2000 and 2003, "The number of Federal inmates held in private facilities has increased over 40%, while the number held in State facilities has decreased 1.8%." The federal government held 21,865 inmates in private facilities at the end of 2003 (Harrison & Beck, 2004, p. 6).

In sum, between 1995 and year-end 2003, the number of inmates housed in for-profit prisons increased nearly 500 percent. In terms of regional dominance, the southern portion of the United States has the highest number of prisoners in both public and private prisons, whereas, echoing the pattern that existed during the operation of the Convict Lease system, the Northeast has failed to implement prison privatization anywhere near the extent of the South (Figure 1.6). Table 1.3 shows that racial disparity in for-profit prisons exists as well. By 2003, the private corporations constituted America's fourth largest prison system, as depicted in Figure 1.7.

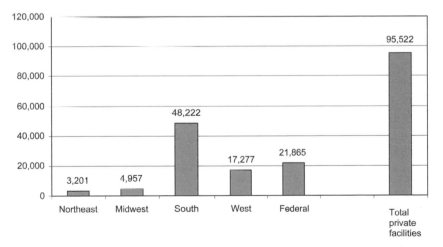

Figure 1.6 Number of state and federal prisoners housed in private facilities by U.S. region, 2003. Source: U.S. Department of Justice.

Table 1.3 Prisoners in Federal, State, and Private Adult Correctional Facilities by Race or Ethnicity and United States region (June 30, 2000).

	Total	White, non-Hispanic	Black, non-Hispanic	Hispanic	Asian/American Indian	Pacific Islander[a]	Not reported
Total	1,305,253	453,300	587,300	203,700	13,240	9,670	37,930
Federal[b]	110,974	29,800	44,800	33,200	1,640	1,480	0
State	1,101,202	395,637	506,408	151,810	9,968	6,527	30,852
Private	93,077	27,905	36,066	18,728	1,634	1,662	7,082
Region[c]							
Northeast	171,999	44,367	86,207	37,872	435	885	2,233
Midwest	233,993	103,374	115,423	10,165	2,721	849	1,461
South	518,912	177,668	279,531	49,417	2,006	759	9,511
West	269,375	98,113	61,313	73,084	6,440	5,696	24,729

[a]Includes Native Hawaiians.

[b]Federal total was estimated based on Federal Justice Statistics data for Sept. 30, 2000, and rounded to the nearest 100 for whites, blacks, and Hispanics, and to the nearest 10 for American Indians/Alaska Natives, Asian/Pacific Islanders, and not reported categories.

[c]Regional breakdowns exclude prisoners in Federal prisons.

Source: U.S. Department of Justice, Bureau of Justice Statistics, Census of State and Federal Correctional Facilities, 2000, NCJ 198272 (Washington, D.C.: U.S. Department of Justice, 2003), p. 3, Table 4.

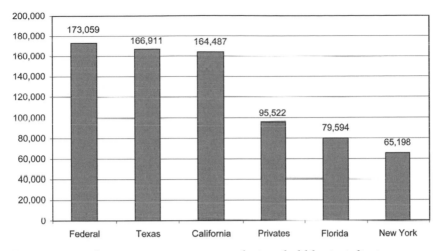

Figure 1.7 Six largest U.S. prisoner populations held by jurisdiction, 2003. Source: U.S. Department of Justice.

The New "Security State": A Note about Hispanic Incarceration

African Americans, of course, are not the only minority group in American society to suffer discrimination. A well-documented bias against non-white, non-Protestant (and even nonmale) groupings of people has existed in America from the beginning (Zinn, 1980). In the United States today Hispanic men also have a far higher likelihood of going to prison than do white males, though this likelihood is still lower than that for African Americans. Although the histories of oppressed groups in the United States are by no means homogenous, these histories demonstrate a common political marginality, a weakened ability to prosper economically, and a greater likelihood of coming under formal state control.

A look at incarceration rates of Hispanic aliens by the U.S. Federal Bureau of Prisons—one of the leading contractors of private prison services—is revealing. First, there has been a dramatic increase in this type of incarceration by the BOP since the mid-1980s, even before September 11th, 2001. In 2000, 87% of Federal defendants charged with immigration offenses were Hispanic (Welch, 2004). By 2003 there were 23,514 BICE detainees (Table 1.4). The dramatic growth in incarceration of immigration offenders, however, began well before September 11, 2001 (Figure 1.8).

Table 1.4 Detainees under BICE Jurisdiction,[a] December 31, 1995, 2000–2003.

Type of facility	Number of detainees					Percent change 2002 to 2003
	1995	2000	2001	2002	2003	
Total[b]	8,177	19,528	19,137	21,065	23,514	11.60%
ICE-operated facilities	3,776	4,785	4,550	5,087	5,109	0.4
Private facilities under exclusive contract to ICE	652	1,829	1,947	1,936	1,935	-0.1
Federal Bureau of Prisons	1,282	1,444	1,276	1,100	1,338	21.6
Other Federal facilities	181	178	162	130	88	-32.3
Intergovernmental agreements	2,286	11,281	11,201	12,812	15,044	17.4
State prisons	8	369	419	453	477	5.3
Local jails	1,984	8,886	8,681	9,764	11,376	16.5
Other facilities	294	2,026	2,101	2,595	3,191	23

[a]On Mar. 1, 2003, functions of several border and security agencies including the U.S. Customs Service and the Immigration and Naturalization Service were transferred to the U.S. Department of Homeland Security, Bureau of Immigration and Customs Enforcement (BICE).

[b]Detail does not add to total because facility type was unknown for one detainee in 2000 and 2001.

Source: U.S. Department of Justice, Bureau of Justice Statistics, Prisoners in 2001, Bulletin NCJ 195189, p. 10, Table 12; 2003, Bulletin NCJ 205335, p. 9 (Washington, D.C.: U.S. Department of Justice). Table adapted by SOURCEBOOK staff.

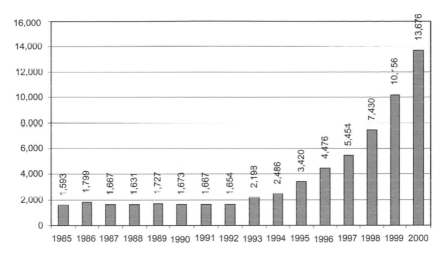

Figure 1.8 U.S. immigration offenders in federal custody, 1985–2000. Source: U.S. Department of Justice.

Dramatic increases in the penalties for immigration offenses have led to a steady increase in the lengths of time served for immigration offenses, a shift from which for-profit prison companies obviously profit. In the aftermath of the events of September 11, 2001, the federal crackdown on illegal immigrants increased all the more. As criminologist Michael Welch states, "Nowadays, with the roundup of Arabs and Muslims, the experience very closely parallels the internment of Japanese Americans. They are people who are easy to identify, and easy to dislike. They're non-white non-Christians in a prevailing American culture that places great emphasis on whiteness and Christianity" (Talvi, 2003; see also especially Welch, 2005). According to Loic Wacquant, a similar pattern could be found throughout Europe before September 11, 2001: "Prison and the branding it effects thus actively participate in the fabrication of a European category of 'sub-whites' tailor-made to legitimize a drift towards the penal management of poverty" (1999, p. 219). Sentence length for immigration offenses increased significantly starting in the early 1990s, from 3.6 months in 1990 to 20.6 months in 2000.

Private Profit, Public Cost: Public versus Private Inmates

Inmates in private prisons are very different entities than their public prison counterparts. Under the auspices of prison privatization, crime and criminals become *engines of private investment* and utilized for local economic development. For shareholders in private prison companies, inmates have quite literally become commodities rather than liabilities. From the perspective of taxpayers, however, inmates and crime are viewed as a state liability—a very real financial burden—competing with other similarly sized items in state budgets such as education, health care, and transportation. As shown in more detail in Chapter 5, the curious mixing of public interests and private stakeholders in for-profit imprisonment has made for some interesting partnerships between powerful government authorities and private prison corporations. In short, the incentive structure associated with for-profit imprisonment dramatically readjusts the crime control formula from attentiveness to crime-reduction strategies to acceptance and dependence upon high crime and harsh punishment for economic viability.

Whereas criminological theories of the past, such as social disorganization theory, sought to identify and mitigate the environmental causes of criminal behavior, newer theories of "routine activities" and "everyday life" seek instead to mitigate risk and "harden targets" (see Felson, 1994). No longer are we actively seeking to address the underlying causes of crime. Instead, criminology is increasingly focused on treating the symptom. This literally "postmodern" shift involves a change in focus for criminology and criminal justice from that of addressing the *causes* of crime to capitalizing on its existence. This is a vitally important change. A recent story by Dow Jones Newswires, for example, noted the private corrections industry as a "safe place to lock away investments" and reported: "Industry watchers predict that the prison population is set to grow due to higher unemployment and tougher law-and-order policies following the September 11 terrorist attacks" (McCarty, 2002, p. 1). Moreover, the U.S. Department of Justice recently announced its official recidivism rate for inmates released in 1994 of 67.5 percent, which, as noted above, the for-profit imprisonment industry views as a boon. In short, as a society we have increasingly given up on the modernist objective of social engineering, except to the extent these conditions can be mitigated for profit by well-connected private entrepreneurs. High crime and imprisonment rates, however, clearly do not serve the interests of citizens or taxpayers.

Finally, another meaningful difference between public and private prison systems is, of course, the profit prison industry's historical attachment to the legacies of colonialism and slavery in the United States. By viewing for-profit imprisonment through the lenses of America's racial history, past and present crackdowns on "Negro" crime, and capitalism itself, this book raises serious questions about the continuing role of race in the operation of the criminal justice system and the larger social agendas behind it (see also Garland, 1996; Rusche & Kirchheimer, 1968; Welch, 2002, 2005). As noted by critical race theorists, attention to details regarding the historical development of social institutions and practices is a vital part of the work necessary for a comprehensive understanding of modern events (L. A. Williams, 1998; Cottrol & Diamond, 1995).

This book offers an alternative view of imprisonment in society today—a view that questions the instrumentalist "crime-control" version of incarceration. Rather than achieving crime control, the disproportionate and targeted use of imprisonment for some groups over others reinforces and perpetuates existing disparities in social life and leaves the underlying causes of crime unaddressed, serving the interests of those who would seek to capitalize on its existence.

Fortress America: Globalization, Privatization, and the New Security State

So, how did all of this come about? What forces led to the renewed vitality of for-profit imprisonment? The reemergence of "privatized" prisons in the twenty-first century has taken place within an important geopolitical context. First, the traditional power of the nation-state is weakening, with economic alliances transcending national borders and ignoring traditional forms of sovereignty and self-determination. Second, the industrialized market economy of good jobs and high wages is following the same path of diffusion. And third, work itself—the relation of labor to capital—is changing as well. The realities of wages, security, and American nationalism are all changing rapidly in a global economy and a world newly threatened by terrorism (Gold, 1995; Frank, 2000; Melman, 2001; Welch, 2004). During periods of intense social change, crackdowns on minority groups are historically quite common (Gusfield, 1963).

Privatization agendas appeal to a broad spectrum of constituents who increasingly want to remove themselves from the earlier agenda of the welfare state while capitalizing on public fear. Programs designed to assist citizens are being replaced with newly invigorated "security-state" programs that have a global reach (Welch, 2004). This prioritization of market-based solutions to social problems corresponds with decreasing state commitments to maintaining social welfare programs and the political salience of cutting taxes (Gold, 1995). But all of this pre-dates September 11, 2001.

Beginning in 1980s America, "Changes in demography, in stratification and in political allegiance, led important sections of the working and middle classes to change their attitudes towards many 'welfare' policies—to see them as being at odds with their actuarial interests and as benefiting groups that were undeserving and increasingly dangerous" (Garland, 2001a, p. 76). In short, over the past twenty-five years, spending on social welfare programs and governmental benefits has been scaled back, while spending on military and criminal justice "security" programs has remained steady or increased (Beckett & Sasson, 2000a). Affinity for corporate welfare for the airline, steel, and agricultural industries, however, remains intact (Frank, 2000).

Private corporations in the areas of policing and corrections have boldly sought to fill state-based gaps in service, in recognition of the fact that consumers (including state and local governments) are seeking to devolve governmental criminal justice functions to private vendors. American corrections firms are vying for contracts in Iraq and Israel, Ireland and South Africa—within a *global* market for incarceration and "security" services. British based SecuriCor, the GeoGroup (formerly known as Wackenhut Corrections Corporation), and Corrections Corporation of America are all firms newly profitable in the area of global "security services." Former president of Corrections Corporation of America Doctor Crants ("Doctor" being his name, not his title) is now president of Homeland Security Corporation (HSC). He is a graduate of West Point. The opening words to his bio on the HSC Web site read:

> Doctor R. Crants founded Homeland Security Corporation in 2001 to provide highly specialized security management training to government and commercial entities. Its training division, PPCT Management Systems, Inc., is an internationally recognized authority on use of force and self-defense training for criminal justice agencies, the military, and corporations.

HSC listed contracts in 2003 with the CIA, FBI, Secret Service, Department of the Army, John F. Kennedy Special Warfare School, Department of Defense, and many others. "Homeland Security Corporation (HSC) provides highly specialized security management and training services to government and commercial entities" (http://www.about-hsc.com/).

The trend toward spending more on security and less on social welfare has only been exacerbated by September 11 and the war in Iraq. The irony, of course, is that it is still all taxpayer money that is paying for everything—"public" or "private"; the difference lies in who directly profits from the expenditure. The recent reorganization of the federal government to include the former Immigration and Naturalization Service, newly renamed the Bureau of Immigration and Customs Enforcement (euphemistically known as "ICE"), under the umbrella of the Department of Homeland Security directly links together incarceration and immigration policies (see Welch, 2004). The U.S. Federal Bureau of Prisons is one of the fastest-growing arms of the federal government. In fact, "The US Department of Homeland Security is expanding a national prison system that detains immigrants facing possible deportation. The current population of about 22,000 detainees represents the fastest-growing segment of the federal prison population" ("U.S. Expanding Prisons," 2003).

As for-profit mechanisms of social regulation expand globally, the populations on which this type of profit is made possible are once again becoming more obviously disfranchised—"invisible"—embodying the kind of voicelessness characteristic of the dispossession of apartheid and early versions of transportation: in sum, those who are politically weak, potentially threatening, economically powerless, and socially reviled. In the United States, as documented in the statistics already presented, this dispossession affects people of color and "aliens" in far greater proportion than whites.[2] Populations of disfranchised people have once again become the targets of private, multinational, corporate entrepreneurship, much as they did in the nineteenth century (see Chapter 2).

In Great Britain, for example, the *London Times* reported on May 15, 2002, that "tens of thousands of destitute asylum seekers will be held in up to 15 large for-profit accommodation centers planned for rural areas of the country" (Ford, 2002). Or take, as another example, in South Africa recently (Africa News Service, 2002), the 3,024–bed Kutama Sinthumule Maximum Prison, one of the largest prisons in the world, that was opened by "a consortium known as the South African Custodial Services Pty Ltd made up of the US-based Wackenhut Corrections and their South African partners, Kensani Corrections Pty Ltd" (Africa News Service, 2002). Alternatively, take, for example, this recent headline from Australia: "Woomera Detainees Sew Lips Together." "At least 58 asylum seekers have sewn their lips together during a hunger strike at the Woomera detention center. The asylum seekers also threw rocks at security guards trying to assist those who had mutilated themselves, seriously injuring one guard. . . . It's understood the detainees are upset at the time being taken to process their visa applications" (Larkin, 2002).

Theoretical Base: Critical Criminology, Critical Legal Studies, and Critical Race Theory

As mentioned above, this book draws upon a well-developed tradition in critical criminology—one that questions the utility of mass imprisonment and the legitimacy of the argument that imprisonment really controls crime. This section provides a brief introduction to the theoretical underpinnings of this book. The information offered here is merely a primer on these schools of thought and not a comprehensive overview. The text below does provide, however, an important synopsis of key propositions relevant to this research offered by several leading critical scholars that will be of interest to readers.

Critical Criminology

Critical criminology is rooted in the "conflict" perspective of sociology, which views social relations in terms of groups vying for social power. Instead of working together in a consensual fashion for the common good (what is called the "consensus view"), groups with unequal power and competing interests constantly battle for control over access to resources, prestige, and political entrée (Bernard, 1983). Although mainstream criminology is often said to adopt a consensus view of the law-making process—that groups have their interests equitably recognized through the mechanisms of representative government on a level playing field—the conflict view asserts that power imbalances subvert consensus. In the conflict view, what really determines outcomes are the *power* and entrée some groups have relative to that of others, with more powerful groups defining "crime" and enforcing law (see Quinney, 1974).

The criminologist noted earlier, Thorsten Sellin, who completed pivotal early work linking imprisonment and slavery, was in fact a leading conflict theorist. His book *Culture Conflict and Crime* (1938), documents how cultural differences among groups lead to broader conflict in society, particularly those societies in which diverse groups of people are thrown together by virtue of colonization, expanding immigration, or advancing urbanization. Specifically, Sellin suggests that the differing "conduct norms" of diverse groups living in shared territory often set them against one another. "Primary cultural conflict" occurs when one group comes to dominate another and where the norms of a smaller cultural group come under the control of a larger, more powerful group, such as in the process of colonization (pp. 62–67). "Secondary culture conflict" takes place when one cultural group that is growing in power emerges with conduct norms differing from those of the dominant culture, such as the mores of diverse ethnic groups regarding use of alcohol or gambling (105–7). In each case, differences in *social power* determine both the functioning of law and the definition of crime based on the values of the dominant culture. Thus, according to the conflict perspective, inequalities in social power are ultimately a real source of what gets defined as "crime."

As discussed in Chapter 2, the dominant white southern majority was successful in redefining previously petty crimes as felonies after the Civil War, thus elevating the penalties for vagrancy, loitering, and petty theft. In his book *Slavery and the Penal System* (1976), Sellin documents how by legislatively mandating lengthy prison terms for behaviors that were previously dealt with through fines and short stints in jail, southern white cultural elites devised a new system of de facto black slavery, the Convict Lease system.

Although conflict theory has undergone several additional iterations, its essential argument, as popularly summarized by Vold, Bernard, and Snipes, remains the same today: "Those with less power are more likely to be defined as criminal and those with more power are less likely" to be defined as such (1998, p. 246).

"Critical criminology" is an offshoot of conflict theory because it recognizes and seeks to explain the creation and application of law, particularly as experienced by groups lacking in power. Early work in critical criminology focused heavily on economic (Marxist) explanations for the power imbalances between "classes" of people (Quinney, 1977). According to these early works, economic imbalances best explained the power-laden enforcement of law by the rich against the poor, with particular attention to how crimes of the wealthy seem never to get as much attention or punishment as the crimes of the poor (see Reiman, 2004). The critical criminology of today, however, is more expansive in its examination of power imbalances and looks at specific cases associated with race, class, and gender (DeKeseredy & Schwartz, 1996; Vold et al., 1998, p. 260; Schwartz & Friedrichs, 1994).

Critical criminologists not only are focused on power imbalances in society but also seek to be reflexive about the inherent power relationships that exist in the process of research itself (see Dekeseredy & Schwartz, 1996; Schwartz & Friedrichs, 1994). In an oft-cited summary, Marty Schwartz and David Friedrichs summarize that modern critical criminology is "characterized particularly by an argument that it is impossible to separate values from the research agenda, and by a need to advance a progressive agenda favoring disprivileged peoples" (1994, p. 222).

Critical criminology has thus evolved from its early focus on economics as the primary source of group inequality to now include examination of the class, racial, patriarchal, and colonialistic social relations that *enabled* the economic exploitation described by earlier critical criminologists. The exploitation of capitalism, from this perspective, involved pre-existing hegemonies of gender and race relations that structured Western society. The capitalistic exploitation focused on in Marxist analyses actually involved deeper sets of oppressive relations including patriarchy, racism, and gender inequality. Today, multiple and overlapping sources of inequality (often called "intersections") are seen to operate simultaneously and are the focus of critical criminology.

Finally, whereas two leading critical criminologists, DeKeseredy and Schwartz, suggest that "by the 1980s, radical criminology was succeeded by critical criminology" (1996, p. 54), Vold et al. (1998) lump "radical" and "critical" criminologies together. They suggest that both "critical" and "radical" criminologies are radical "in the sense that they are associated with political agendas that involve deep and fundamental change" (p. 260). In fact, Vold et al. use "radical" and "critical" criminology interchangeably. Other scholars note the difficulty of pinning down with precision any absolute definition of critical criminology beyond that associated with research exploring the use of power and its oppressive consequences for some groups (Bierne & Messerschmidt, 2000, p. 198; Schwartz & Friedrichs, 1994). For the purposes of this book, "critical criminology is defined as a perspective that views the major sources of crime as the class, ethnic, and patriarchal relations that control our society" (DeKeseredy & Schwartz, 1996, p. 239).

Thus, the building blocks of earlier critical criminological work are still being utilized in research today; however, they are merely the foundations of today's critical scholarship. Take, for example, the work of Katherine Beckett and Theodore Sasson (2000b) and their recent research on racism in the drug war titled: "The War on Crime as Hegemonic Strategy: A Neo-Marxian Theory of the New Punitiveness in U.S. Criminal Justice Policy."

Or take as another example James Messerschmidt's text *Capitalism, Patriarchy, and Crime: Toward a Socialist Feminist Criminology* published in 1986, in which he blends Marxist traditions with the insights of feminist scholars of violence against women in the home. John Hagan (1989) began to explore patriarchy and gender role socialization within the family to explain the juvenile crimes of sons versus daughters. Today, critical criminology devotes itself more and more to exploring how these overlapping oppressions interact, contribute to, and exacerbate the social experiences of oppressed groups. In a democratic society, knowing and understanding all of the complex dimensions of inequality is essential for achieving liberty and justice for all.

Critical Legal Studies and Critical Race Theory

In much the same way that critical criminology began with a narrow focus on only one primary type of (capitalistic) oppression and developed beyond this to include examinations of racial, class, and gender issues as well, a movement in the sociolegal studies arena, the so-called critical legal studies (CLS) movement also evolved over time to expand its research agenda to include multiple sources of oppression as well. The critical legal studies movement provided central underpinnings of the still emergent critical race theory movement (see Gregory, 1987). Moreover, just as it is difficult to find definitions of Critical Criminology that are agreed upon by all self-described critical criminologists, real differences of opinion among proponents of critical legal studies exist as well—even as a diverse range of scholars purport to be engaged in this work (see Balkin, 1991).

The primary assertion of the critical legal studies movement regards the limitations of a reliance on formal legal "rights" to ensure social equality among individuals of various groups (Mench, 1998). Most CLS scholars agree that the starting place for their work involves criticism of the classical belief in the ideal that democracy embodies a "rule of law over the rule of men." CLS questions the notion that law is applied equally in a democratic society. The classical view of law is flawed and inaccurate: "Law is, in this conception, separate from—and 'above'—politics, economics, culture, and the values or preferences of judges or any person. In this separation resides the law's ability to be objective, principled, and fair" (Kairys, 1998, p. 1). In liberal legal traditions, supposedly the law applies to every citizen, and no citizen is above the law. From a critical race theory perspective, however, we can start our examination of law by pointing out that the worst crimes in human history have almost always been *legal* at the time they were committed—and invariably committed against groups of people who were politically marginalized and socially reviled (Lopez, 1995; Cottrol & Diamond, 1995; Zinn, 1980).

In short, according to proponents of critical legal studies, having "rights" on paper by no means guarantees equal justice (see Kairys, 1998). The study of law must be approached from a perspective of "realism," CLS scholars say, which involves incorporating a sense of "politics" into our understanding of how law actually works. To view law as a neutral instrument of objective fairness is patently naive, in the CLS view. The research of CLS scholars, therefore, explores limitations to the liberal view of law by documenting the discriminatory operation of law *in practice.* Western law, in CLS research, is well documented as being far from objective, often unfair, and saturated with power politics from its earliest patriarchic conceptualizations. The operation of law, in fact, is inundated with forms of privilege associated with patriarchic (male), classist (rich), and racial (white) history going back to the founding of the country. As with the evolution of critical criminology, critical legal studies began with a concentration on its subject in a narrow formulaic fashion ("legal rights") and later expanded its examination of justice to include racial and gender dynamics in the operation of law.

Much of the work by early CLS scholars took place in the late 1970s in august settings like Harvard Law School and, to a somewhat but not altogether lesser extent, the University of Wisconsin at Madison (see Crenshaw, 2002). Whereas early CLS research was dominated by scholars who happened to be white and male, later work emphasizing race and gender has come to the fore and been undertaken by a more diverse set of scholars. In a very real way, the critical race theory movement began during offshoot conversations at CLS conferences among scholars wanting to get more specific about the different types of exclusion they were observing. Critical race theory specifically questions whether reliance upon a liberal "rights-based" tradition will ensure equality for *minority* groups. To quote Richard Delgado, a leading critical race theorist: "Virtually all of Critical Race thought is marked by deep discontent with liberalism, a system of civil rights litigation and activism characterized by incrementalism, faith in the legal system, and hope for progress, among other things" (1995, p. 1). Critical race theorists have been discontented with an overreliance on belated enforcement of minorities' civil rights in American society, arguing that deeper and more fundamental changes are necessary for equality to be achieved.

A leading critical race theorist, Kimberle Crenshaw, chronicles the evolution of critical race scholarship in a number of works and documents the tumultuous beginnings of what she describes as the "race turn in CLS," which began at academic conferences devoted to critical legal studies. Feminist CLS scholars (known as "femcrits") were particularly interested in expanding discussions of race and gender at CLS meetings and asked: "What is it about the whiteness of CLS that keeps people of color at bay?" (2002, p. 1355). The answer to this question partially involves the fact that few faculty members in the CLS movement were minorities or females who could give voice to concerns of racial and gender oppression—and, in their early days, those who did tended to be students rather than faculty members.

As expanded discussions of race and gender emerged, meetings are described as being fractious and divisive. Conversations about race and gender within the CLS movement were accompanied by serious battles among faculty fighting for academic positions and vigorous debates about the objectives of sociolegal scholarship (see Gregory, 1987).

Drawing on the tradition of critical legal studies, critical race theory views "liberal" reliance upon strictly legal remedies to social injustice as insufficient and naive. Such faith in law is seen as "legal ideology" rather than "legal realism," with researchers from the critical legal studies and critical race theory traditions documenting historical examples of law being used by powerful groups against the interests of less powerful, particularly minority, groups (Mench, 1998; Crenshaw, 2002).

Most important, critical race theorists note that identity markers of race, class, and gender have historically been associated with oppression—so much so they argue that racial, classist, and gender identity status markers such as "white," "rich," and "male" are *part and parcel of the mechanism of oppression*. In other words, rather than simply pointing out—as traditional "liberal" scholars have—that social injustices tend to follow clear racial, class, and gendered patterns, critical race theorists emphasize the political power of identity categories themselves, particularly racial identities. Specifically, "whiteness" and masculinity are empirically, socially, culturally, and historically associated with access to power and wealth, whereas "darkness" and femininity are associated with powerlessness, poverty, and—increasingly—imprisonment (Burns,

1998; Kennedy, 1998). *Social injustices, therefore, are associated with these identity markers, and rather than being simply measurable by-products of an oppressive system, social identity markers associated with race, class, and gender are themselves mechanisms of oppression.* That is, ideas about the appropriateness of men versus women pursuing certain occupations, whites versus blacks belonging to particular social clubs or organizations, and working-class people attending particular elite universities all have powerful effects on social expectations and social relations. That American society has been historically dominated by European systems of thought and power is a fact often revisited by critical race theorists (L. A. Williams, 1998; Hill-Collins, 1991).

The important point is that as the femcrits began to organize and gain power, the importance of articulating various types of oppression became apparent. Being female and being black, for example, clearly involves multiple and overlapping types of oppression that can be experienced simultaneously. A focus on race and rights that did not include the dynamics of gender in the operation of power was incomplete. As Crenshaw explains the evolution: "Feminist legal theory laid claim to a broader undertaking than a mere study of rules governing sex discrimination: Contained within the broader feminist concept was the project of unpacking law's relationship to gender. What would be the parallel concept for critical scholars of color seeking to lay claim to the broader study of law's relationship to race?" (2002, p. 1360). Here, critical race theory, according to Crenshaw, was born.

> Turning this question over, I began to scribble down words associated with our objectives, identities, and perspectives, drawing arrows and boxes around them to capture various aspects of who "we" were and what we were doing. The list included: progressive/critical, CLS, race, civil rights, racism, law, jurisprudence, theory, doctrine, and so on. Mixing them up and throwing them together in various combinations, one proposed combination came together in a way that seemed to capture the possibility we were aiming to create. Sometime toward the end of the interminable winter of 1989, we settled on what seemed to be the most telling marker for this particular subject. We would signify the specific political and intellectual location of the project through *"critical,"* the substantive focus through *"race,"* and the desire to develop a coherent account of race and law through the term *"theory."* (pp. 1360–61; emphasis added)

According to black feminist Patricia Williams, in order to comprehensively address the multiple and overlapping sources of inequality experienced by varying types of individuals, an "alchemy" of sorts will have to be embraced—and this requires a spiritual openness and a willingness to risk the safety of previously held certainties for the purposes of exploring democracy (1995). According to today's views of CLS and critical race theory, looking only at rights constrains a research agenda that should include stories about how law is experienced by different groups and what law "means" to various people (Hill-Collins, 1991; P. J. Williams, 1991, 1995; Walker, 1982; hooks, 1992, 2000; Kairys, 1998; C. West, 1993; Scheingold, 1991; Yngvesson, 1997; Turk, 1995). Only then are we exploring the true functioning of law, how it really operates in the lives of people and how it is perceived (or not) among groups with differing levels of social power.

In her book *Black Feminist Thought: Knowledge, Consciousness, and the Politics of Empowerment* (1991), Patricia Hill-Collins discusses the political nature of all social "identities" and the importance of viewing the sources of oppression through multiple lenses. Collins notes, as well, that oppression may be experienced differently by members of the same racial group: "Members of the black middle class, most of whom became middle class through social mobility from working-class origins, may express more ambivalence concerning their function as controllers of working-class blacks" (p. 60). Cornel West explains the connection, then, between critical race theory and critical legal studies in the concluding essay of *The Politics of Law:* "The CLS movement is significant primarily because it introduced for the first time in legal discourse a profoundly historicist approach and theoretical orientation that highlights simultaneously the brutal realities of class exploitation, racial subordination, patriarchal domination, homophobic marginalization, and ecological abuse in the American past and present" (1998, p. 714).[3] "Are legal institutions crucial terrain on which significant social change can take place?" asks West. Yes and no. Although "existing legal apparatuses" are incapable of "adequately" or "substantially" transforming social injustice, the enterprise of attempting to remedy past inequities through legal venues "remains indispensable" (p. 708).

Legal victories are thus seen by critical scholars as necessary but not sufficient for achieving lasting progressive social change. At the same time, successful efforts to transform American society through legal venues will likely be short-lived and scaled back by subsequent (capital-driven) conservative victories in the courts won by powerful interests. In short, however, localized social movements, grassroots politics, and engaged citizens who understand the word *democracy* as a *verb* rather than a noun are what is required to transcend the limitations of our liberal (rights-based) legal tradition. Grassroots activism and the encouragement of public storytelling is vital to achieving this kind of citizen engagement—through music and culture, through public lectures and meetings, and through scholarship as well (Olivas, 1995; Oberweis & Musheno, 2001).

To be ultimately effective, critically minded activists must anchor their work in the public sphere. In the words of CLS scholar David Engle, "I reject socio-legal models focused on law's capacity to dominate everyday life or everyday life's capacity to resist the hegemony of law. Instead, I draw upon a perspective that emphasizes the mutually constitutive processes through which law and everyday life construct one another" (1996, p. 126; see also Sewell, 1992).

Finally, an important and still emerging issue relevant to the development of critical race theory is the criticism leveled by many that it too heavily relies on a "Black/White paradigm" for its exegesis of social oppression.

> The Black/White paradigm signifies the reduction of race relations in American society and law to relations between "white" Euro-Americans to "black" African Americans. Consequently, this paradigm ignores or denies the existence and relevance of persons hued with other colors, such as Asian Americans, Native Americans, and Latinas/os. In addition, this paradigm marginalizes even persons who are hued white or black but who derive from cultural or geographic destinations other than Europe or Africa, such as persons from Caribbean nations, who identify as both black and Latina/o. (Inglis Thomson, 1997, p. 1647n8)

In much the same way, Stuart Henry and Dragan Milovanovic have been arguing for a critically oriented "constitutive criminology":

> The core of our constitutive argument is that crime and its control cannot be separated from the totality of the structural and cultural contexts in which it is produced. It rejects the argument of traditional modernist criminology that crime can be separated from that process and analyzed and corrected apart from it. Crime is an integral part of the total production of society. It is a co-produced outcome of humans and the social organizational structures that people develop and endlessly rebuild. Analysis of crime must relate crime to the total societal picture, rather than to any single part of it. (1999, p. 7)

As mentioned earlier, this book is derived from my experiences working with activists in a grassroots effort to stop or scale back corporate and state attempts to "privatize" state prisons in Tennessee and elsewhere (see Hallett & Lee, 2000). This book is very much a product of my shared experiences "in the world" fighting for my beliefs. What happens in "everyday life" reveals much about how notions of "law" and "order" affect legal action. In our new global context, the marginalized are more and more among us.

Agenda

Chapter 2, "For-Profit Imprisonment in American History," explores the operation of the Convict Lease system in the aftermath of the Civil War. The chapter shows how the Convict Lease system in the American South determined the early social understanding, structure, and operation of inmate labor by utilizing dislocated slaves as its primary source of revenue. While compelling large numbers of former slaves back into agrarian labor, the Convict Lease system also expanded the use of forced labor into "industrial" pursuits such as railroad construction and coal mining (Lichtenstein, 1996). As such, the Convict Lease system not only reestablished white power over large numbers of emancipated slaves but also enabled northern industrialists to capitalize on the oppressive race relations of southern society by exploiting a newly created population of wage-free laborers (Curtin, 2000; Lichtenstein, 1996).

Three ominous similarities between the justification of for-profit imprisonment in the postbellum South under the Convict Lease system and the private prison industry of today are further examined here: first, the social construction of a "Negro crime problem" after the Civil War; second, a dramatic corresponding rise in the incarceration rate of African Americans; and third, the existence of a well-connected cabal of for-profit "entrepreneurs," willing and eager to develop means of private profit through incarceration (see Curtin, 2000). The racial dimensions of the modern for-profit imprisonment industry must be examined for what they still represent: a racialized mercantilism of imprisonment disproportionately concentrated in the South and disproportionately reliant upon young black men as its primary source of economic production.

Chapter 3, "Capitalist Crime Control: Social Disorganization as Market Opportunity," explores the racial dynamics of modern prison privatization in the United States from the perspective of social-disorganization theory. This chapter relies particularly on the concepts of "social" and "human" capital to suggest that the social conditions leading to the mass incarceration of mostly minority males in the United States are the *very same forces creating economic opportunity for the private prison industry:* social dislocation, joblessness, failing schools, familial dissociation, and residential transience. Due to late-twentieth-century imprisonment policies, a renewed understanding of prisoners as commodities has emerged, transforming inmates from a population worthy of help and rehabilitation in the 1960s and 1970s to a commodity used by private entrepreneurs and even state and local governments for economic development today.

By specifically targeting impoverished communities such as Youngstown, Ohio, for example, with promises of jobs in already destitute labor markets, private prison corporations thrive on the very conditions social-disorganization theorists identify as the *cause* of crime. This chapter reveals how the explicitly racial character of advertisements for Corrections Corporation of America seek to capitalize on critical tensions surrounding issues of social welfare and crime. Increased rates of residential transience even in middle-class suburbs, changes in the structure of the employment market, the prevalence of crime imagery and violence in the news and entertainment media, and heightened fear of crime overall combine to generate support for repressive measures of crime control that ignore larger questions of social justice while promoting ever sacred profit seeking (Garland, 2001a).

Chapter 4, "Money and Power: The Political Economy of For-Profit Prisons," expands the discussion of modern prison privatization to examine arguments about the "prison industrial complex." Although the notion of a "prison industrial complex" is certainly useful for understanding many of the interesting parallels between massive cold war–era defense budgets and the post–cold war prison budgets of today (that is, fear of communism and communists versus fear of crime and criminals), the Eisenhower-era euphemism for a "war economy," as Susan Blankenship and Ernest Yanarella point out, has also been applied to "agriculture (agri-business complex), transportation (auto-highway-petroleum rubber complex), energy (atomic-industrial complex), medicine (medical-industrial complex), social policy (health-education-welfare complex)" and even professional sports, as by critics of public financing of stadiums and professional sports franchises (2000, p. 14).

Whereas the "military industrial complex" was driven by a well-defined and identifiable interest group seeking to expand the Pentagon's annual budget and military programs from the "top down," the "crime complex" supporting the expanded use of incarceration is much more diffuse and supported more by state and local interests, from the "bottom up" as it were, than by the federal government (Parenti, 1999, pp. 213–14). Criminal justice, after all, is primarily a state and local enterprise—even though the 1994 Violent Crime Control and Law Enforcement Act, for example, offers federal subsidies for state prison construction. Most prisoners, however, are sent to state prisons and local jails by state and local officials "with different agendas, constituencies, incentives, and constraints" rather than by representatives of the federal government (Greenberg & West, 2001, p. 618).

Although private prisons have certainly been promoted as a tool for economic development, far more than just economic interests are served by what David Garland calls the "crime complex"—that combination of social, political, economic, and cultural forces that hold "crime control" in continuously high prominence as a social issue (Garland, 2001a). Crime and criminality are a central part of American popular culture. Garland lays out several elements of what he calls the "cultural formation of the crime complex" that help explain mass imprisonment (p. 163):

- high crime is regarded as a normal social fact
- emotional investment in crime is widespread and intense, encompassing elements of fascination as well as fear, anger, and resentment
- crime issues are politicized and regularly represented in emotive (emotional) terms
- concerns about victims and public safety dominate public policy
- the criminal justice state is viewed as inadequate or ineffective
- private defense routines are widespread and there is a large market in private security
- a crime consciousness is institutionalized in the media, popular culture, and the built environment

In short, as Eric Schlosser states in his *Atlantic Monthly* article titled "The Prison Industrial Complex": "The prison industrial complex is not only a set of interest groups and institutions. It is also a state of mind" (1998, p. 73). The interconnections among public, private, political, economic, and cultural correctional agendas constitute a "crime complex" vast enough to both engender and explain the massive public investment in incarceration experienced over the past twenty-five years without the existence of a top-down cabal of self-interested actors. As will be shown in Chapter 5, however, this does not mean that self-interested actors are not active in the arena of for-profit imprisonment—quite the contrary, to be sure. That said, however, the "military industrial complex" metaphor as applied to imprisonment in the United States breaks down under close scrutiny. The problems of hyperincarceration in our society are even more deeply and locally rooted in our culture and history than any top-down capitalist or government conspiracy. This does not mean, of course, that capitalists will not seek to capitalize on these preexisting cultural sentiments.

As shown in the second half of this chapter, however, private prison entrepreneurs rely heavily on localized connections with varying spheres of influence and access in the policy arena. No two contracts are the same or authorized by the same authority. The specific connections necessary to enable and authorize a private prison contract vary dramatically by jurisdiction. *In many ways, the localized ambitions of prison entrepreneurs are more insidious than any federal-level Pentagon contract because they are foisted onto smaller, more vulnerable jurisdictions* (such as local sheriffs or city councils), often lacking in sophistication regarding contract monitoring, negotiation, and enforcement. Time and again, small city- and county-level officials find themselves in tough negotiations seeking to enforce terms of contracts they understood to be agreed upon (see Gilbert 2000b).

Chapter 4 concludes with a detailed case study of the interconnections and personal relationships among several governmental and private stakeholders who actively promoted the 1997 initiative to privatize the entire Tennessee state prison system and the "subgovernmental" status of the major players involved. The events described here reveal a key truth about for-profit imprisonment: that for-profit imprisonment is often made possible through networks of private and public stakeholders that are less accountable and indeed less visible to citizens than their public prison counterparts. These networks involve combinations of private and governmental authorities that render imprisonment a *proprietary* ("private") rather than a *public* good. Indeed, during the public hearings exploring the cost-effectiveness of CCA's proposed takeover of the entire Tennessee prison system, CCA's consultant to the state legislature delivered portions of his report in closed hearings to the oversight committee, stating that the information was "proprietary."

Citizens wanting to cross-examine the information put forward by CCA for management of a public prison were denied the opportunity to do so, because the information was deemed equivalent to a "secret of trade" (see Hallett & Lee, 2000).

Chapter 5, "Bad Faith: A Critical Look at 'Faith-Based' Corrections," establishes the racial context of American criminal justice policy in current public debates about crime, welfare, and incarceration. As noted by Currie, between 1985 and 1995, the number of African Americans sentenced for drug crimes increased by 700 percent (1998, pp. 12–13). Specifically, by drawing on literature exploring status politics and social movements, chapter 5 examines "faith-based" correctional initiatives as a "symbolic crusade" orchestrated by "moral entrepreneurs" determined to reduce taxes for the wealthy while simultaneously blaming the poor for their "immoral" behavior. As such, traditional governmental responsibility for addressing the causes of crime is sidestepped, and "personal accountability," "faith," and "morality" are placed at center stage. By constructing the crime problem as an issue of morality and personal religious faith, activists promoting this devolutionary agenda ignore the structural disadvantages faced by many of the "Godless" allegedly needing salvation. Given the disproportionate minority representation in prison populations, the faith-based prison movement equates faithfulness with conformity and, by connotation, faithlessness with misconduct. As shown in this chapter, the explicit connection between faith-based programming and prison privatization lies in their shared relationship to the agenda for "welfare reform" and a scaling back of the welfare state for the "undeserving poor."

By examining this latest trend in criminal justice privatization, the so-called faith-based corrections movement, this chapter documents racial shifts in public "crime consciousness" that help explain current willingness to again privatize prisons. The chapter outlines the social context of privatization by placing it in the framework of "welfare reform" and the broader conservative movement aimed at reducing governmental assistance to the poor while dramatically increasing spending on prisons. The chapter concludes with a cross-examination of the claims made by proponents of private faith-based corrections programs and compares them to the academic evidence on crime causation and the ecological distribution of crime.

Chapter 6, "The Easy Inmate Market: The Micropolitics of Private Prisons," lays out several basic policy questions relating to prison privatization generally, including an analysis of its current scope, some of the budgetary and overcrowding forces driving its adoption, and an assessment of the evaluation data regarding the performance of privatized prisons to date. This chapter's discussion illustrates how debate surrounding prison privatization in state legislatures is typically devoid of any discussion of race—but is focused, instead, on lesser issues of contract management and evaluation of public versus private prison performance. Although several religious denominations have come out with position papers decrying the exploitation of prisoners for profit, these concerns have by and large been absent from the public debate. Associated with contemporary privatization efforts is a host of "micromanagement" issues that have, unfortunately, become the central points of debate about the merits of for-profit incarceration: cost-effectiveness, evaluation and contract-monitoring strategies, inmate classification criteria, and measurement issues. Such micromanagement issues have also tended to dominate legislative and academic dialogue on the subject of private prisons, while discussion of racial concerns and the history of the industry has been muted and confined to more activist circles (Hallett & Lee, 2000).

As this chapter shows, however, a strong argument can be made that private prisons have broadly failed to live up to their promise, even in terms of the micromanagement issues put forward on their behalf. If, as the U.S. General Accounting Office (and many others) point out, large-scale savings have not been generated by prison privatization, why does it continue to be considered (Austin & Irwin, 2001; Abt Associates, Inc., 1998; U.S. General Accounting Office, 1996)? Since privatized control over prisons reemerged in the mid-1980s, numerous prison contracts between private companies and jurisdictions of all sizes (federal, state, and local) have been terminated for either lack of performance or outright abuse (Abt Associates, Inc., 1998; Camp & Gaes, 2000a, 2002). Nevertheless, at this writing, several states and the federal government are considering or have recently enacted expansive prison privatization contracts, with the number of prisoners in private prisons today at an all-time high at 95,522 inmates (James, 2002; Welch, 2005).

The practice of imprisonment, critical criminologists believe, is only indirectly related to "crime control," while also governed by other forces such as unemployment, preexisting imbalances in social power, and ideological sentiments about punishment or vengeance or fear of crime (see Garland, 1990; Foucault, 1977). In order to understand imprisonment, therefore, one must look beyond "crime control" as its primary explanatory variable. As David Garland puts it: "Punishment today is a deeply problematic and barely understood aspect of social life, the rationale for which is by no means clear" (1990, p. 3).

Finally, Chapter 7, "Commerce with Criminals. The New Colonialism in Criminal Justice," suggests criminal justice policy is currently at a critical juncture in regards to mass incarceration. The for-profit imprisonment industry has capitalized on the rhetoric of fiscal conservatism and the ideology of law-and-order politics without having to match up rhetoric with reality. This chapter demonstrates how the private financing of prisons has enabled politicians to simultaneously "get tough on crime" without having to overtly raise taxes (Dyer, 2000). Should public confidence in massive social expenditures for prisons begin to erode, as we are beginning to see in many jurisdictions such as California, Michigan, and Illinois, the easy inmate market could dry up very quickly.[4] As revealed in a recent news report about a CCA prison in Youngstown, Ohio:

> A privately operated prison seen as an economic boost for the area has announced 200 layoffs, about 45 percent of its 449–member staff, and more cuts could be ahead. The reductions in the Northeast Ohio Correctional Center, operated by the Corrections Corporation of America of Nashville, Tennessee, reflect a declining inmate population, the company said. An additional 50 to 100 workers might be laid off if the inmate population drops more, Warden Brian Gardner said yesterday. (Sangiacomo, 2001)

Popular recognition of the fact that the private prison industry is a house the drug war built, based largely on the overincarceration of non-violent minority offenders and fed by the overlapping interests of many stakeholders, may help amplify calls for a movement in decarceration. Related calls for more fiscally responsible use of government resources can effectively be tied to calls for less use of expensive and ineffectual prisons. The cultural politics of for-profit prisons are thus seated on a fault line between two competing agendas of modern conservatism (not necessarily bounded by political party): first, the broadly writ goal of reducing the size of governmental expenditures and, second, the task of exploiting hard-line criminal justice policies for political gain. Although this fault line has held steady for many years, recent developments in the United States foretell shifts in policy alignments that could make agendas for fiscal conservatism become the unwitting accomplice of reductions in the use of prisons (mass incarceration, after all, has hardly resulted in less governmental expenditure). This development could render the for-profit imprisonment industry a bygone experiment, instructive as much for its weaknesses as for the tenacity of its appeal. Fewer private prisons at this writing, however, seems, to borrow a phrase, a forlorn hope (Sullivan, 1990).

TWO

For-Profit Imprisonment in American History

Although the history of forced servitude of captives involves many eras, cultures, and societies, in the United States this servitude has almost exclusively been imposed upon people whose ancestry is traceable to Africa. As Cornel West points out:

> The African slave trade was sustained by profit-hungry elites of all kinds: Christian, Muslim, Jewish, European, Arab, African and American. Yet the distinctive feature of New World slavery was its "racial" character. After a few decades of transracial slavery—in which whites, blacks, and reds were owned by whites—this ancient form of subjugation became an exclusively black and white affair. (1999, p. 51)

That the Thirteenth Amendment authorized the creation and use of for-profit imprisonment in the United States irrevocably ties for-profit imprisonment to the issue of race in America—and is an

American juristic reality of which many today remain unaware. A real contribution of the work of philosopher Cornel West is documentation of the genealogy of racism in America (see 1999, 1998, 1997, 1993). Specifically, West argues that a key *enabler* of racism is public ignorance of history.

West documents three "white supremacist logics"—"the battery of concepts, tropes and metaphors constituting discourses that degrade and devalue people of color" that have negatively impacted all people of color in American society, albeit in different ways and to different degrees:

> *Judeo-Christian racist logic*—tracing "the biblical account of Ham looking upon and failing to cover his father Noah's nakedness, thereby provoking divine punishment in the form of blackening his progeny";
>
> *Scientific racist logic*—"which promotes the observing, measuring, ordering, and comparing of visible physical characteristics of human bodies" of the sort the so-called "father of criminology," Cesare Lombroso, engaged in; and
>
> *Psychosexual racist logic*—"This logic is rooted in Western sexual discourses about feces and odious smells—relates racist practices to bodily defecation, violation and subordination, thereby relegating black people to walking abstractions, lustful creatures or invisible objects. All three white supremacist logics view black people, like death and dirt, as Other and Alien." (1999, pp. 263–64)

Imposing identity attributions on people based solely on their skin color obviously constitutes racism. Through work done on the project of mapping the human genome, the concept of *race* itself has been proven to be bankrupt and scientifically invalid. Notions about race are social constructions devoid of any objective scientific legitimacy. Indeed, as Ian Haney Lopez points out about the genetic variation between individuals of different skin colors in his contribution to the book *Critical Race Theory:* "Greater variation exists *within* the populations typically labeled Black and White than *between* these populations. These findings refute the supposition that racial divisions reflect fundamental genetic differences. . . . Race must be viewed as a social construction" (1995, pp. 194, 199; emphasis in original).

Race, Colonialism, and the Rise of Penology

Utilizing the labor power of captives has been a strategic objective of state authorities for centuries of human history (Sellin, 1976). That the Thirteenth Amendment simultaneously abolished slavery and initiated forced "involuntary servitude" for convicts in the United States dramatically speaks to this duality in the American context. Profit motive with prisoners, in short, is hardly a new innovation. Jeremy Bentham, designer of the famed "Panopticon," very much viewed himself as a private prison entrepreneur who "expected to become rich" from his architectural "prison management" scheme (Feeley, 2002, p. 332). Indeed, the circular Panopticon itself was intended to be a cost-efficient means of a enabling a small number of guards to supervise a large number of convicts by way of its design. Much of Bentham's writing on the Panopticon, in fact, is actually in the form of a *contract proposal* for the administration, construction, and management of his Panopticon or "inspection house," in which he flatly states: "To come to the point at once, I would do the whole by contract" (quoted in Bozovic, 1995, p. 51).

Bentham's self-titled "plan of management" relied on the use of contractors who would manage the inmates in the Panopticon prison for a profit—with Bentham holding a patent and monopoly on the venture (ibid.). At Auburn Penitentiary in 1828, the prison administration "announced its confidence that no further appropriations would be needed from the State for maintenance," due to the profitable use of prison labor (Lewis, 1967, p. 131). Bentham developed his model of inspection not just for prisons but also for "houses of industry," "poor houses," hospitals, manufactories, madhouses, and schools (Bozovic, 1995, p. 51). Each of these schemes relied on, as Bentham put it, "the apparent omnipresence of the inspector (if the divines will allow me the expression), combined with the extreme facility of his real presence" (p. 45). As Feeley points out, in Great Britain, the prospect of cost savings generated by efficient use of the Panopticon by private contractors was its primary attraction to authorities, because such a prison "could be run as a business venture" at little or no cost to the state (2002, p. 332).

Prior to the implementation of the prison as a punishment in its own right, the practice of "transportation"—the shipping of convicts and debtors (who were also convicted criminals) to North America to work on colonial tobacco or cotton plantations—had already proven cost-effective for the Crown (Feeley, 2002, pp. 327–29). Only with the American

Revolution and the demise of transportation did the prison "become synonymous with punishment" in England. "Within 50 years, the prison was so well inscribed in public imagination and so well established on the landscape, that it was impossible to envision criminal punishment in its absence" (p. 330). The demise of transportation left the state with the need for an alternative mechanism through which to manage large numbers of prisoners, and the privately managed prison was presented as a reasonable option. As Bentham put it to his potential British clients: "What hold can any other manufacturer have upon his workmen, equal to what my manufacturer would have upon his? What other master is there that can reduce his workmen, if idle, to a situation next to starving, without suffering them to go elsewhere?" (Bozovic, 1995, p. 71).

In short, private commerce in human beings caught up in the criminal justice system has been under way for centuries in Anglo societies dating back to the 1600s. This commerce has generally involved the prospective use of captives' labor to reduce or eliminate imprisonment costs. Transportation, a practice *developed* and *proposed* by private merchant shippers in seventeenth-century England, literally involved "transporting" convicted but pardoned criminals to North American plantations for periods of indentured labor. Transportation greatly expanded the sanctioning power of the state at little or no cost, because it relied on private entrepreneurs (Feeley, 2002). As a result, an entire criminal justice process for management of large numbers of captives became routinized for the first time.

In addition to this penal traffic in laborers were large numbers of "free" and mostly white indentured servants, who generally for the cost of passage would, after being officially pardoned for a criminal offense in many cases, submit "voluntarily" to transportation and a period of indenture (usually from four to seven years) (Smith, 1965, pp. 89–135). "Actual shipment of the convicts was performed by merchants trading to the plantations. . . . [T]he merchants made their profit by selling the convicts as indentured servants in the colonies" (pp. 97–98).

Without question, then, one of the key forces driving these "innovations" in criminal justice policy was British colonial imperialism. In the case of transportation, colonial use of convict laborers was thought a commonsensical solution to the problems of crime and listlessness in Great Britain—as well as a useful means of expanding British influence abroad at little or no cost to the Crown (Feeley, 2002; Smith, 1965). These white indentured servants, however, were keenly distinguished from "Negro slaves": this multiracial assembly of people subject to differing forms of servitude "were variously known as indentured servants, redemptioners, or, in order to distinguish them from the Negroes, as Christian or white servants" (Smith, 1965, p. 3). As the colonies became more established and stable, many "free" people sold themselves into indenture for the cost of passage, after being convicted and pardoned for vagrancy or property crime convictions if they agreed to be transported (pp. 43–66).

After the Revolution and the end of transportation, American need for workers, of course, persisted—especially as the supply of white indentured labor dwindled. The abolition of transportation thereby exacerbated the importance of slavery in colonial America, where "society was not democratic and certainly not equalitarian; it was dominated by men who had money enough to make others work for them" (Smith, 1965, p. 7). The racist doctrine of "white supremacy" conveniently began to thrive during this period, with the exploitation-derived benefits of the African slave trade quickly surpassing those of white indentured servitude:

> Negro slaves, of course, answered many colonial requirements even better than did white servants. Slaves were held to perpetual instead of temporary servitude, they were usually cheaper to feed and clothe, they replaced themselves to some extent by natural breeding, and they endured the hot climate of the plantation colonies much better than white men. Hence the use of Negroes did in actual fact do away with the economic demand for white servants in those colonies which found them suitable. . . . Planters would no longer go down to the shore and buy from a servant ship, though they eagerly took up the shipments of Negro slaves which arrived. (pp. 29–30)

The Convict Lease System

Neither slavery nor involuntary servitude, except as a punishment for crime whereof the party shall have been duly convicted, shall exist within the United States, or any place subject to their jurisdiction.

—Thirteenth Amendment, Constitution of the United States

After the Revolutionary War, the agrarian economy of southern plantation society increasingly depended upon the exploited labor of captive Africans—as it did until and beyond the abolition of slavery itself. The agricultural production mechanisms of the time were labor intensive, requiring large numbers of workers to till, plant, harvest, process, transport, and refine products. The abolition of slavery potentially destroyed the relations of production necessary for southern economic survival. After the Civil War, however, former slaves were no longer legally subject to forced servitude as the private property of their "owners." Furthermore, many able-bodied white workers had been killed or maimed during the war, and white servitude in the form of indentured labor had ceased to exist as well. This combination of factors created a massive labor crisis in the postbellum South, creating the need for the Convict Lease system.

This labor crisis was felt not only by plantation owners facing the prospect of having to *pay* laborers a prevailing wage but also by emerging industrialists desperate for low-cost workers. The social and economic elites of the "New South" (be they industrial or agrarian) needed a mechanism through which they could abide by the legal tenets of abolition while maintaining their exploitative power over a large class of vulnerable and needed workers—namely, the now free but indigent former slaves still populating the South.

Although in many respects the Civil War was fought over the increasing dominance of an industrialized versus traditional agrarian economy during a time of profound economic and social transition, the Convict Lease system emerged to serve the interests of both industrial entrepreneurs and the still powerful agrarian planter class. The fulcrum of this systematic forced labor exploitation after the Civil War, for both classes, was the ideology of *white supremacy.* Anchored as it was in the legal authorization of the Thirteenth Amendment, the Convict Lease system ironically perpetuated a system of racialized forced agrarian labor precisely at the time it was to legally have ended. "Virtually all blacks were labeled 'laborers,' and the architects of the Convict Lease system never intended that black and white should mix. As early as 1866 planners decreed it 'not only important—but vital' that the races be kept separate in any penal institution in the 'new order of things'" (Ayers, 1984, p. 198). "It was wrong, in other words" writes Edward Ayers, "to imprison together white murderers and a black who had stolen a pig—it was unjust to the whites" (p. 199). An additionally important facet of Convict Leasing is that it expanded forced labor beyond feudalistic-style agrarian slavery to include modern industrial pursuits such as coal mining, railroad construction, and logging run by for-profit entrepreneurs (see Lichtenstein, 1996; Shelden, 2001; and Colvin, 1997).

Without question, the predominant numbers of convicts sentenced to involuntary servitude under the Convict Lease system were African American former slaves (Lichtenstein, 1996; Mancini, 1996; Colvin,

1997). Although systematic empirical records for the South as a whole are lacking, the clear pattern emergent from state and local records is that, after the Civil War, the African American incarceration rate increased dramatically. "Before the Civil War," writes Ayers, "virtually all the prisoners had been white," whereas after the Civil War "about nine out of ten were black" (1984, p. 197). "Under slavery the prisoners in Alabama's penitentiary," for example, "were 99 percent white. But after emancipation the vast majority of prisoners were black" (Curtin, 2000, p. 6). By 1890, "in the entire state of Alabama, whites comprised less than 4 percent of all prisoners" (p. 2).

The forced servitude of black prisoners during the operation of the Convict Lease system still differed in important ways, however, from the *slavery* conditions of the antebellum South, in both positive and negative respects (Curtin, 2000; Lichtenstein, 1996; Mancini, 1996). First and foremost, the legal justification of forced labor under the Convict Lease system had, of course, changed the public rationale of involuntary servitude: prisoners subjected to forced labor under the lease system were still, ostensibly at least, punished as a consequence of their own "freely willed" illegal behavior—and not as a result of their "inferior" human condition. Second, as historian Mary Ellen Curtin points out, whereas "southern slavery was a violent institution that undoubtedly bequeathed certain traditions that shaped the treatment of prisoners," many convicts released from servitude at the end of their sentences lived the rest of their lives in freedom. Things *had* begun to change. Convict laborers in the coal mining industry, for example, often went on to work for wages in the very same mines to which they had been introduced as slaves (2000, p. 19). This is not to pronounce the Convict Lease system virtuous by any means, but to illustrate how complex and *real* was the southern dependence upon forced labor.

Curtin, for example, relates instances of large groups of free black men walking into town courthouses in Alabama and casting their votes collectively as early as 1868. "Even if a frightened black voter had been tempted to break ranks and run, his fellow squad members would not have allowed it" (p. 37). Freed slaves now had the rudiments of formal legal rights, which they used frequently to defend themselves from trumped-up charges or withheld wages and to uphold the right of independent commercial enterprise. This agency on their part did not free them from the racism of southern society at large. Nevertheless, "freedmen" collectively pressed for their rights to a fair wage, to rent land at a fair price, and to "make fair labor contracts" upheld by law—and they began to recognize the power of their numbers at the polls, particularly in all-important county-level elections, where freed slaves were often the numeric majority (pp. 35–37).[1]

At the same time, however, convict laborers cannot be considered simply members of a new working class. Slavery-era racism and the ideology of white supremacy saturated the operation of the Convict Lease system to its core. As historian Alex Lichtenstein documents in his book about Convict Leasing, *Twice the Work of Free Labor: The Political Economy of Convict Labor in the New South:* "The use of black convicts in southern industry reflected the refusal by many whites to accept the ideological tenets of emancipation and free labor relations, even in an economy undergoing transformations brought about in part by the destruction of slavery. The lessees regarded black labor as a commodity inseparable from the convicts themselves, much as slaveholders had regarded slaves" (1996, p. 21). In short, the Convict Lease system perpetuated the *racialized* system of forced labor necessary for the survival of the agrarian planter class, while also accommodating the industrial development of the New South. In short, owners of railroads, coal mines, and logging companies were equally interested in exploiting imprisoned African Americans as were plantation owners (see Lichtenstein, 1996; and Mancini, 1996).

"New South Slavery": The Racist Foundation of Convict Leasing

> The prevalence of the lease system in former slave states lends credence to the common view that the postbellum southern penal system could be traced to the legacy of slavery, a tradition of black forced labor that could not be dislodged by emancipation and Reconstruction. Yet, without denying the significance of this continuity, it is important to recognize that the Convict Lease was far more than just a functional replacement for slavery. . . . Convict labor depended upon both the heritage of slavery and the allure of industrial capitalism.
>
> —Alex Lichtenstein, *Twice the Work of Free Labor*

In any normally functioning supply-and-demand ecosystem, situations of high demand and low supply result in higher costs. According to the most naive and basic tenets of American capitalism, in the aftermath of the Civil War, freed slaves should have been able to command a wage for their desperately needed labor. Indeed, the foundational strategy of "free labor" itself involves the ability to negotiate fair contracts, to share information, and ultimately to leave oppressive work situations in search of better opportunities. Without freedom, workers literally become captive to the whims and profit motives of their employers. It is important to realize, therefore, that the transition in forced labor from slavery to the Convict Lease system in the United States was "not simply a replacement for slavery," but a *new form* of racially distinctive coerced labor practice serving many of the same interests as slavery and new interests as well (see Colvin, 1997, p. 200). Presupposing a (nonexistent) democratic free market, conditions were right for black workers to gain influence. In reality, however, the racist exploitation and political suppression of blacks continued. As Mark Colvin writes: "Control of the black labor force was a constant goal of the southern punishment system since the Civil War. This labor control function was *enhanced* with the rise of industrialism in the 'New South' rather than eliminated" (1997, p. 265; emphasis added).

Thus, despite the presence of well-established southern penitentiaries expressly devoted to rehabilitation and solitary confinement during the period in question, the Convict Lease system soon dominated southern punishment after the Civil War. The racial difference in prisoners between northern and southern penitentiaries before and after Emancipation is striking and unequivocal. Ayers reports that after the Civil War, "the racial composition of the Southern prison population had changed radically overnight. Before the Civil War, rural counties sent few people to the penitentiary; in the postbellum era, black belt counties became major suppliers of the state penal apparatus" (1984, p. 197). Although most histories of the penitentiary in the United States emphasize the role of penance, silence, and productive labor for inmates, this formula was quickly abandoned in the South with the advent of Convict Leasing. According to Ayers, before the Civil War, the penitentiary model spread "almost simultaneously" throughout the North and South (p. 34). Afterward, in the South, this tradition was ignored. In response to this sudden shift, criminologist Mark Colvin muses: "A most illuminating question is not why the convict leasing system and chain gangs predominated in the South, but why these forms of punishment did not develop in the North. If economic motives were only in play, these forms of punishment would certainly have been adopted in the North: they were less expensive and far more profitable than any other penal system developed in the nineteenth century" (1997, p. 264).

This "leasing" of inmates to for-private-profit entrepreneurs across the South, therefore, helped resolve several "crises" for southern society not paramount in the North. Each of these crises also hinged directly or indirectly on the issue of race. First, Convict Leasing maintained the slavery-era tradition of white control over large numbers of black laborers. Second, the Convict Leasing system was *adaptable* to both the land-driven interests of the remaining agrarian planter class as well as the industrial and capital-driven businesses of the New South (such as coal mining, logging, turpentine production, and, especially, railroad construction) (see Lichtenstein, 1996, pp. 1–16). Third, Convict Leasing kept alive a distinctive *social* hierarchy that made Convict Leasing subjectively more difficult to challenge from below. In other words, keeping white supremacy alive had its own sort of legal *and* social utility: convict laborers were not to consider themselves potential political or economic equals to their overseers.

Prior to Emancipation many southern industrial markets were operated with wage workers at significantly higher costs than would be the case under Convict Leasing. As Lichtenstein describes what he calls "New South slavery," the Convict Lease system facilitated a legal form of "industrial slavery" by maintaining and capitalizing upon the preexisting exploitation of African American labor on farms and plantations and capitalized on three factors then operating in unison (1996, pp. 1–16): "an isolated labor market, cheap labor, and repressive social and race relations" (p. 12; see also Mancini, 1996; and Colvin, 1997). *All three were necessary for the Convict Lease system to emerge,* as perhaps best evidenced by the absence of the lease system in the North (Colvin, 1997). Thus, the system helped relieve southern states of massive war-era debt by providing laborers for a society totally dependent on manual production for its wealth. Companies leasing inmates from the prison systems of the South also added much needed capital to state treasuries, whereas maintaining inmates in the solitary confinement of a penitentiary offered states a fiscal liability. In addition, much of the southern infrastructure was decimated during the war, including many government buildings, courthouses, and even penitentiaries themselves, making it impossible to physically house the large numbers of black inmates being sentenced regardless (Mancini, 1996, pp. 13–58; Lichtenstein, 1996, pp. 1–16, 37–72).

The important point, of course, is that confining the new population of black "criminals" in penitentiaries was not the objective of what Ayers calls "the new order" of things: perpetuating the exploitation of black labor was the objective (1984, p. 198). Although the punishment of crimes committed by slaves was not a concern of the criminal courts during slavery—this was undertaken by masters—after Emancipation, the courts were flooded with "Negro" criminals. As W. E. B. Du Bois explains: "Throughout the South, laws were immediately passed authorizing public officials to lease the labor of convicts to the highest bidder. The lessee then took charge of the convicts—worked them as he wished under the nominal control of the state. Thus a new slavery and slave trade was established" (2002, p. 85).

Finally, and most ominously, the Convict Lease system got wide social support for its supposed success in controlling and punishing what was to be defined as the first-ever "black crime problem" (Curtin, 2000, pp. 42–61). With total disregard for the economically destitute position in which freed slaves found themselves after the war, many southern whites militated for escalating punishments associated with the dependency crimes committed by blacks. Writing about the exponential increase of black prisoners in Georgia after the Civil War, Alex Lichtenstein notes: "The rapid increase to over one thousand prisoners by 1880 was due almost solely to the long-term convictions meted out to blacks, a trend which would continue for decades. Ten year sentences for burglary, for example, were not uncommon for African-Americans" (1996, p. 59). Consequently, southern black prisoner populations skyrocketed in what David Oshinsky calls a "flood of criminals" (1996, p. 3). Edward Ayers documents the rise of white versus black convicts after 1865 in five southern states, as shown in Figure 2.1 (1984, 180).

"Worse Than Slavery": Physical Punishments under Convict Leasing

As the title of one of the classic histories of the Convict Lease system conveys, the prevailing attitude of many private contractors to whom prisoners were leased was callous and profit driven: *One Dies, Get Another*. Matthew Mancini's title comes from a quote of a private contractor lamenting the criticisms leveled against the Convict Lease system by humanitarians and labor organizations: "Before the war, we owned the negroes. If a man had a good negro, he could afford to keep him. . . . But these convicts, we don't own 'em. One dies, get another." Thus, Mancini characterizes what he sees as the "most salient difference" between the Convict Lease system and slavery not as the technical

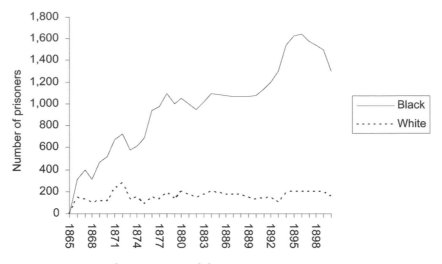

Figure 2.1 Race of convicts in Alabama, Tennessee, Virginia, Mississippi, and Georgia, 1865–1898.

distinction of freedom the new black convicts held before they offended, but the even more torturous physical punishments exacted upon prisoners than upon slaves (1996, p. 3). Without a direct "ownership" interest in the forced laborers under their control, many entrepreneurs felt free to literally work convicts to death. David Oshinsky's book *Worse Than Slavery: Parchman Farm and the Ordeal of Jim Crow Justice* (1996) also deals with the notoriously brutal conditions of Mississippi's for-profit farm-labor system.

Mary Ellen Curtin documents lease projects in Alabama with death rates of "over thirty percent per annum" on the Georgia Pacific Railroad (2000, p. 85), whereas Mancini documents death rates as high as 16 percent in the labor camps of Mississippi (1996, p. 67). In short, the incentive structure operative under the Convict Lease system was oriented toward working men quite literally to their deaths—"pushing every convict to the limit of endurance" (Lichtenstein, 1996, p. 53). Indeed, "the mortality of convict railroad workers contrasted sharply with that of free labor employed at similar work" (p. 54).

Whereas death was a frequent consequence of conscription under convict labor, leased prisoners also endured whipping, "water torture (where one is strapped down, face up, nostrils held shut, with barrels of sometimes boiling water poured down the throat), food deprivation, harsher work assignments, and outright physical torture" (see Curtin, 2000, p. 69; Lichtenstein, 1996, p. 130; and Mancini, 1996, p. 75). "The lash," according to Mancini, "was the most frequently used" punishment by "whipping bosses, a designated agent whose job it was to inflict punishment" (1996, p. 75). These methods were not only directed at the individual convict but also aimed at the group as a whole—to reinforce that subjective perception of legal inferiority to whites, "to keep blacks in their place." As Mancini puts it: "Whipping is a punishment not just of insupportable pain but of deep humiliation as well. Few men or women can bear it in silence. The vulnerability of the recipient and the power of the boss who metes it out are underscored by the ritual nature of the chastisement" (p. 76).[2]

In short, the for-profit status of *leased* rather than owned inmates encouraged an attitude among corporate operators of willing mistreatment. Leasing agents for the coal mines, for example, soon began "classifying" convicts (first, second, third class) according to their ability to meet productivity quotas or "tasks," explicitly endorsing the use of violent methods such as whipping to exact higher productivity (Curtin, 2000, pp. 66, 133–34). "Healthy prisoners cost more than smaller, weaker men and women" (p. 66).

The inability to negotiate a wage or contract, a total lack of control over working assignments and conditions, and the coercive realities of existing solely for the purposes of a *privately* dictated profit motive characterized the experience of convict laborers. Under the Convict Lease system, the state essentially "rented" inmates to private contractors, who were entitled to whip, discipline, and manage them with no oversight from the state. The state, "after receiving a fixed sum, paid little attention to the prisoners while the lessee fed, clothed, guarded, and worked them to his own profit" (Mancini, 1996, p. 15). In a formula that remains the operating basis for the private prison industry today, the incentive structure for the Convict Lease system was to spend as little as possible on inmates in order to keep profits at their highest level.[3]

Capitalizing on the First "African American" Crime Problem: A Precursor to the Modern War on Drugs

An important parallel between the origin of the Convict Lease system in the postbellum South and the private prisons of today is that both systems of for-profit imprisonment were started in response to the same "crisis": escalating and costly inmate populations composed of mostly African American prisoners. As described above, the absolute poverty of African American former slaves caused an increase in property crimes committed by blacks (see Curtin, 2000, pp. 42–61). Curtin documents the helpless position of former slaves when their land-use and working rights were redefined by Emancipation. During slavery, for example, slaves fed themselves for "free" with food *they* grew but did not own from the plantation. With abolition, however, this practice was no longer legal—without a fee—and many blacks long accustomed to feeding themselves from the land of the plantation were arrested and charged with theft (pp. 46–47). Many former slaves were also charged with "trespassing," "vagrancy," or "loitering" as they lingered on plantation homesteads figuring out what to do after Emancipation. Sentenced to long prison terms or fines they could not pay, many were thrown into the Convict Lease system to work the *very same plantations* where they were held as slaves (Shelden, 2001).

As historian Milfred Fierce explains, former slaves "were easy prey for the contrivances of landowners bent on depriving them of their entitled wages" and ultimately their liberty itself (1994, p. 6). Agents of the Freedmen's Bureau, a federal agency created to implement the transition out of slavery, reported "black workers, evicted from farms after the crop had been harvested, wandering the roads starving and naked" (Curtin, 2000, p. 47, quoting letters and accounts of Freedmen's Bureau agents). The frequent occurrence of plantation owners failing to pay their former slaves the wages they were due, however, was deemed a "civil" matter, not subject to criminal prosecution (ibid.). Whereas slavery "justice" was administered privately on plantations, after the Civil War the criminal justice system developed a "preoccupation of police and courts with blacks" (Ayers, 1984, p. 198). As discussed in more detail in Chapter 3, incarceration policies associated with crimes committed disproportionately by blacks in the 1980s, under the auspices of the war on drugs, also resulted in the overcrowded and unconstitutional conditions in public prisons, leading to the 1983 founding of Corrections Corporation of America in Tennessee.

Similarities between Past and Present: The "Negro Crime Problem," Fiscal Prison Crisis, and Entrepreneurial Profit Motive

Alabama's temporary resurrection of the chain gang notwithstanding, contemporary prisons and the nineteenth-century lease share other even more troubling similarities. Prisoners are no longer leased out, but private companies still see convicts as a source of profit. The profit motive, the recent sharp increase in the prison population, and the disproportionate number of incarcerated African Americans link current practice to the past. If the United States is truly concerned that barbaric prison conditions remain in the past, it needs to examine how these three factors shape and corrupt prison operations today.

—Mary Ellen Curtin, *Black Prisoners and Their World, Alabama, 1865–1900*

The "Negro Crime Problem"

After Emancipation, crimes of economic dependency committed by freed slaves increased dramatically. Although the vast majority of these crimes were petty property crimes, they were met with increasingly harsher punishments. As a mechanism of political repression, the criminal justice system of the time was uniquely suited to meet two desperate needs of southern society: (1) a continuation of the racially exploitative labor practice of slavery (declared illegal by Emancipation) to enable (2) recovery from the vast devastation left by the Civil War (Curtin, 2000, p. 55). The "threat of so-called 'Negro criminality'" not only justified the repressive and rapid adoption of the Convict Lease system but also "proved" to whites that black former slaves were "inferior" and in need of repression after the South's defeat in the war (Lichtenstein, 1996, p. 21). *Black crime, in other words, served as the rationale for reinstituting race-based forced labor as well as reasserting white supremacy.* Combined with the economic crisis facing many land-poor whites, states like Arkansas and Mississippi passed nearly simultaneous "pig laws," for example, "which classified the theft of any cattle or swine as grand larceny with a maximum term of five years" for which convicts could be leased to private contractors (Mancini, 1996, p. 120).

Though it would seem counter to the interests of white contractors to brutalize their convicts too excessively, death rates in southern Convict Leasing enterprises far exceeded those of their northern free-labor counterparts working in similar industries. "The desire to drive convicts to their limit, and yet care for them under less than sanitary conditions which might undermine their capacity for hard labor, was a tension that ran through this labor system throughout its existence" (Lichtenstein, 1996, p. 54). This clearly irrational mistreatment is instructive. In addition to the obvious advantages of the continuation of forced labor, the Convict Lease system embodied a cathartic mechanism for the losers of the war as well (see Oshinsky, 1996).

In fact, the unique brutality of the Convict Lease system was not an insignificant element causing its widespread adoption. The establishment of the Convict Lease system occurred so swiftly after the Civil War that many historians characterize it as a rapid departure from the rehabilitative ethic of the penitentiary and "their own penal traditions" (Lichtenstein, 1996, p. 21; see also Ayers, 1984; and McKelvey, 1977). By more harshly criminalizing what were previously petty crimes committed by destitute (but "free") blacks, the southern criminal justice system cathartically reasserted the preexisting social order.

The New "Black Crime" Problem

The dramatic rise in African American incarceration rates in the more recent 1980s and 1990s has similarities with the rise in incarceration experienced by freed slaves after the Civil War. *In both cases, the majority of crimes for which blacks were suddenly imprisoned in disproportionately high numbers were nonviolent petty crimes only recently made "serious" by changes in law.* Prior to the 1980s, drug crime in the United States was dealt with more as a public health concern than as one of law and order (Currie, 1993). With the implementation of the drug war, however, punishment of impoverished black citizens' drug use far outpaced that of whites. By the end of the 1990s, "almost 1 of 3 (32.2 percent) African-American men in the age group 20–29 [were] either in prison, jail, probation or parole on any given day." "Instead of a large, menacing horde of dangerous criminals, our inner cities actually contain a growing number of young men, mostly nonwhite, who become involved in unskilled, petty crime because of no avenues to a viable, satisfying conventional life" (Austin & Irwin, 2001, pp. 3, 46). As Sampson and Wilson point out about New York City in 1980: "Whereas less than 7 percent of poor whites lived in extreme poverty or ghetto areas, 38 percent of poor blacks lived in such areas" (2000, p. 129).

Another important similarity exists between the period ushering in the Convict Lease system and the modern drug war: massive social and economic change. Today in the United States and globally, the influence of the traditional nation-state is becoming more diffuse, with economic alliances transcending national borders and ignoring traditional forms of sovereignty and self-determination. In addition, the formerly reliable industrialized market economy of good jobs and fair wages is following the same path of diffusion. Work itself—the relation of labor to capital—is changing as well. The realities of wages, security, and nationality are in massive flux all over the world. As technology and globalization both shrink and expand the conditions of employment and labor relations for workers, massive transformations in the viability of previously robust industries cause dislocation and a sense of vulnerability among citizens. Such shifts create a sense of what sociologist Emile Durkheim called "anomie" or "normlessness" among people in society.

In his classic work *The Division of Labor in Society*, Durkheim explains that during periods of economic uncertainty and transition, vigorous attempts to reassert the norms and solidarity structures of the faltering social order will surface. Traditional structures and customs dominant in the previous division of labor will tend to be vaunted and reasserted. As industrialization took hold, for example, it fostered less interdependence among people, and a "cult of individualism" emerged that threatened previously reliable social expectations. Punishment, in Durkheim's view, is very much about asserting the normative order and bolstering "social solidarity," particularly during periods of rapid social change. Punishment is always as much directed at the public *audience* as it is at the offender. Though much of Durkheim's theory of punishment has now been dismissed (in part because he failed to fully consider the power relationships involved in the execution of punishments and definitions of crime), his insights regarding "the moral basis of penal law, about the involvement of onlookers in the penal process, about symbolic meanings of penal rituals, and about the relationship of penal institutions to public sentiment" are very much alive in criminology today (Garland, 1990, pp. 27, 23–46; see also Liebling, 2004).

After the Civil War, profound social and economic transformations were being experienced by southern society: sovereignty and economic control had been lost, the foundational agrarian economy was in decline, and new forms of labor relations were determining economic destinies. Arguably as a consequence, just after the Civil War the South rather abruptly abandoned the rehabilitative ethic of the penitentiary system that had been sweeping the country prior to the war (Colvin, 1997). In a similar way, David Garland describes how more recent social and economic transformations in American society led to a shift away from the rehabilitative penal ethic of the 1960s to the more punitive ethic of the 1980s and 1990s. As the 1980s economy softened, larger segments of the working middle class previously supportive of the welfare state abandoned support for social welfare programs and called for "welfare reform."

> Changes in demography, in stratification and in political allegiance led important sections of the working and middle classes to change their attitudes towards many of these [rehabilitative] policies—to see them as being at odds with their actuarial interests and as benefiting groups that were undeserving and increasingly dangerous. . . . These new group relations—often experienced and expressed as highly charged emotions of fear, resentment, and hostility—formed the social terrain upon which crime control policies were built in the 1980s and 1990s. (2001a, p. 76)

By the late 1990s, when official unemployment rates were at all-time lows, incarceration rates for the same period were at record highs. Not coincidentally, both the highest concentrations of unemployment *and* incarceration for the period are found among urban African American men. As suggested earlier, the low unemployment rate of the 1990s was clearly artificially low, illustrating how imprisonment had replaced welfare as one of society's primary means for regulating the poor (Simon, 1993; Western & Beckett, 1999). In short, rather than attempt expanding security through spending on job programs and food stamps, priorities shifted to incarceration, prison construction, and the war on drugs. This sort of retrenchment is characteristic during times of social change (Durkheim 1933), just as it was after the Civil War.

Fiscal Prison Crisis

A second similarity between social conditions at the time of Convict Leasing and today is the fact that the rising numbers of prisoners were causing fiscal crises associated with the costs of housing inmates. In fact, the world's largest-ever private prison company, Corrections Corporation of America, was formed when a federal court declared Tennessee's overcrowded prison system unconstitutional in the mid-1980s. Like many states in the late 1970s, Tennessee began its own crusade to implement mandatory minimum sentencing and fight the drug war. Predictably, this resulted in tremendous overcrowding and led to a federal court order placing caps on the state's prisoner population. By 1985 the situation reached a crisis point, with rioting and several deaths and the declaration of the state's oldest prison at Nashville unconstitutional. As a result of this court order, Tennessee found itself very quickly in need of at least seven thousand additional prison beds and called for spending $380 million to build six new prisons (Tennessee Select Oversight Committee on Corrections, 1995). It was during a special legislative session called to address the state's prison overcrowding crisis that a cofounder of CCA, Tom Beasley, introduced CCA's first-ever proposal to manage a statewide prison system (Hallett & Lee, 2000). Said businessman Beasley in 1985:

> Our proposal is simple—we will pay the state for the right to manage the system under the state's supervision; we will spend private capital to improve the system and draw our profit out of more efficient use of the state's regular operating budget. That is a $250 million—one quarter billion dollar turnaround in the state budget—without a tax increase! We believe this is absolutely a win-win situation and an unprecedented opportunity to make Tennessee a leader in this most difficult area. (Corrections Corporation of America, 1985, p. 2)

In a similar way, Curtin documents how financial exigency drove the adoption and expansion of the Convict Lease system of Alabama in 1875. State coffers, severely reduced by war-related losses and a failing economy, were still being drawn upon to fight "negro crime" (Lichtenstein, 1996, p. 21). "Money earned from prison labor was then placed in the state's treasury as revenue. Profits . . . soon amounted to between eleven and twelve thousand dollars . . . over and above all the expenses of the institution. At a time when the state desperately needed revenue without new taxes, [the state's new prison warden, John G. Bass] transformed Alabama's penitentiary into a profitable moneymaker" (Curtin, 2000, p. 66).

Entrepreneurial Profit Motive

Finally, the presence of politically well-connected "entrepreneurs" willing to experiment with the profitability of managing mostly black prisoners is another striking similarity between the Convict Lease system of the past and the for-profit prisons of today. Tom Beasley, cofounder of CCA, was also a former head of the Tennessee Republican Party at the time of his proffer to the state. Beasley, therefore, had close connections to then governor Lamar Alexander, also a Republican, who embraced the use of private prisons and considered leasing the entire state prison system to Beasley on a ninety-nine-year lease (cooler heads prevailed in the state legislature) (Hallett & Lee, 2000). Numerous other interconnections between CCA and the Tennessee state government are documented in Chapter 5.

In a similar way, one of the founding wardens who developed the Convict Lease system in Alabama, a man whom Jane Curtin calls "the architect of the modern lease system," John Hollis Bankhead, went on to become a U.S. senator with backing from the very railroads and coal mining industries to whom he once supplied laborers (Curtin, 2000, p. 200). Lichtenstein documents businessmen in Georgia with connections to Convict Leasing who worked hard to make the lease a political and legal reality: "Mark A. Cooper—one of the proponents of convict leasing in 1866—was one of Georgia's more prominent iron entrepreneurs of this era, and believed wholeheartedly in the possibilities of southern industrialization based on coal and iron ore deposits" (1996, p. 110).

Modern-day financiers also regularly speculate on the profitability of private prisons (Schlosser, 1998; Bates, 1998). A recent press release from Dow Jones Newswires suggested private prisons are a "safe" place to invest during times of economic volatility and downturn. Quoting several financial analysts from around the country, the story reveals much about the forces driving the contemporary industry in for-profit prisons: "Industry watchers predict that the prison population is set to grow due to higher unemployment and tougher law-and-order policies following the September 11 terrorist attacks" (McCarty, 2002).

In addition to using prisoners as a method of generating investment wealth, many jurisdictions see private prisons as a source of regional economic development. In a recent story from Mississippi, "Private Prisons Fill Void Left by Plant Closings," several laid-off workers express gratitude for their CCA job at the Delta Correctional Facility in Greenwood: "With the plant closings we've had, it has been the key to our success" (Harden, 2002). As mentioned above, southern use of convict labor was also very strongly supported because of its economic utility.

As an aside, the Convict Leasing–era practice of ranking inmates according to their profitability has a parallel with today's private prisons as well, where modern profit-driven imprisonment firms also place a premium on certain types of inmates, in this case, however, preferring the most docile, healthy, and nonviolent of all inmates because they are cheaper to guard and easier to manage (Camp & Gaes, 2000a; Hallett & Hanauer, 2001). As has been well documented, the modern private prison industry prefers low-level, nonviolent drug offenders, the characteristic subject of drug-war policies (Austin & Irwin, 2001; Camp & Gaes, 2002).

Conclusion: Slavery's Legacy

As the largest of bloodstains on American history, the war between the states was in many ways *the* defining American moment, both for its catechism of equality and the long path we still follow today in pursuit of it. The doctrine of human equality as the source of human freedom is the hallmark American value, expressed most directly perhaps in the Declaration of Independence itself.[4] In modern times, entrepreneurial profit making with convicts has reemerged in concurrent appearance with a new population explosion in African American prisoners during a period of deep level social change and economic transition. As noted above, this reappearance has striking similarities with the past. During both periods, well-placed entrepreneurs were on hand to devise means of profiting from high rates of incarceration that involved disproportionately high numbers of minority prisoners. In speaking about how merchant shippers strategically planned to "raise a cargo" of human beings for shipment to North America (and who worried that the "market" would dry up for fear of peasant emigration), Abbot Emerson Smith explains the shippers asserted the following dictate to sponsors: "Yet the fact is that most people have always been poor and exploited, and nevertheless have rarely emigrated. On the contrary, it has usually been only with the greatest difficulty that people, no matter how miserable their condition, have been persuaded to cut loose from their ancient moorings and try a new country" (Smith, 1965, p. 43).

THREE

Capitalist Crime Control: Social Disorganization as Market Opportunity

Punishment is neither a simple consequence of
crime, nor the reverse side of crime, nor a mere
means which is determined by the end to be
achieved. Punishment must be understood as a
social phenomenon freed from both its juristic
concept and its social ends. We do not deny that
punishment has specific ends, but we do deny that
it can be understood from its ends alone.

—Georg Rusche and Otto Kirchheimer,
Punishment and Social Structure

This chapter explores the racial dynamics of contemporary prison privatization in the United States from the perspective of social-disorganization theory. It relies particularly on the concepts of "social" and "human capital" to illustrate how, due to late-twentieth-century imprisonment policies, a renewed understanding of prisoners as *commodities* has surfaced in criminal justice policy. Specifically, this chapter argues that the social conditions leading to the mass incarceration of mostly minority males in the United States are the very same forces creating economic opportunity for private prison firms: social dislocation, unemployment, failing schools, residential transience, and familial entropy. Particularly because of enforcement policies targeting a narrow spectrum of drug use, a transformed understanding of prisoners has emerged that has changed inmates from a population worthy of help and rehabilitation in the 1960s to a per diem *unit of commerce* viewed by private entrepreneurs (and state and local governments) as mechanisms for economic development today.

By specifically targeting impoverished communities such as Youngstown, Ohio, for example, with promises of jobs in already derelict labor markets, private prison corporations now thrive on the very conditions that social-disorganization theorists have identified as the *cause* of crime. As the for-profit imprisonment industry sells itself, increased rates of geographic transience, changes in the structure of the employment market, the prevalence of crime imagery and violence in the news and entertainment media, and a heightened fear of crime overall combine to generate support for repressive measures of "crime control." As support for these repressive measures builds, responsibility for helping people displaced in deteriorating neighborhoods is shifted away from the public sphere of government and increasingly into the private sphere of "markets" (Garland, 2001a). As part of this discussion, the explicitly racial character of advertisements for Corrections Corporation of America and how they seek to capitalize on tensions surrounding issues of race, social welfare, and crime to promote for-profit imprisonment must be examined. As shown in the advertisements presented here, this privatized shift in social responsibility is touted as moral, natural, and positive for schoolchildren—with Corrections Corporation of America being a source of religion, neighborhood safety, and sound business strategy.

Crime, Racism, and Poverty: White versus Black Crime Rates

Race plays a prominent role in several areas of criminal justice functioning today, ranging from racial profiling by police officers prior to arrest to racial disparities in the likelihood of being sentenced to prison (R. Kennedy, 1997). As William Chambliss, past president of the American Society of Criminology, writes: "The poor, especially urban poor African-Americans, are disproportionately the subjects of law enforcement activities at all levels, from arrest to imprisonment" (2001, p. 67).

The debate about black incarceration rates being the product of higher black crime rates is addressed by the recent work of Franklin Zimring and Gordon Hawkins (1997) and others (for example, Mann & Zatz, 1998; and

Lynch & Patterson, 1990). Not only in terms of victimization by crime but also in terms of other key areas such as level of education, household income, infant mortality, and longevity itself, African Americans fare far worse than whites (Shaw & McKay, 1969; Chambliss 2001; Currie 1993; Wilson & Herrnstein, 1985). According to the U.S. Bureau of Justice statistics: "A black male in the United States today has a greater than 1 in 4 chance of going to prison during his lifetime . . . and a white male has a 1 in 23 chance of serving time" (Bonczar & Beck, 1997, p. 1). U.S. black males represent the single most populace group under correctional supervision in proportion to their population, rising steadily from 5.2 percent in 1985 to 9.0 percent in 1997, with 13.4 percent of black males ages twenty-five to twenty-nine in prison or jail by the end of 2001 (Maguire & Pastore, 2002, table 6.2). The evidence documenting structural biases negatively impacting the life chances of African Americans is overwhelming (see Wilson, 1996, 1999). Without question, the life chances of African Americans are far more constrained than those of whites (Wilson, 1999).

In terms of violence, research has shown for decades that Americans in general, *regardless of race,* commit more violent crime than their G8 counterparts, and that differences in violent crime rates between whites and blacks in America are not as great as the difference between white Americans and Europeans (Zimring & Hawkins, 1997, pp. 21–50). In fact, *white Americans* have much higher violent crime rates than population averages for other G8 countries and comparable property crime rates. As Zimring and Hawkins point out, violent crime is thus an "American" problem, not a racial problem unique to American blacks (1997, pp. 51–72). Moreover, long-standing ecological research on crime and victimization going back to the 1930s work of Clifford Shaw and Henry McKay in Chicago thoroughly documents that *lower-class whites have higher crime rates than middle-class blacks* (1969). Shaw and McKay's research showed definitively that much crime is a function of neighborhood conditions and not race. Those who dismiss structural explanations for criminality seem also willing to disregard (or to simply ignore) findings demonstrating the comparatively high violent crime rate of *whites* in the United States. That it took equivalent comparisons of black Americans' crime rates to white Americans' crime rates before we could dismiss the racial presumption about higher black criminality is also instructive regarding the power of racism in the criminal justice system (Mann & Zatz, 1998; C. West, 1999).

Finally, although poor whites have higher crime rates than middle-class blacks, the criminality of poor blacks and whites cannot be considered equivalent phenomena involving a shared experience of "social disorganization." As Shaw and McKay put it:

> The important fact about rates of delinquents for Negro boys is that they too, vary by type of area. They are higher than rates for white boys, but it cannot be said that they are higher than rates for white boys in comparable areas, since it is impossible to reproduce in white communities the circumstances under which Negro children live. Even if it were possible to parallel the low economic status and the inadequacy of institutions in the white community, it would not be possible to reproduce the effects of segregation and the barriers to upward mobility. (cited in Lauritsen & Sampson, 1998, p. 67)

Although white boys growing up in disadvantaged neighborhoods not only have higher crime rates than middle-class black boys, they do so without having suffered the same oppressive and segregationist racial experience. We may conclude from this that both poverty and racism each contribute, in different ways, to generating the kinds of social disorganization associated with criminal behavior in our society. In the latest study of social disorganization and crime in Chicago, two prominent scholars found again that "poverty was the single most important factor to influence the level of disorder in the Chicago neighborhoods studied" (Sampson & Raudenbush, 2001, p. 4).

Imprisonment and Social Capital

A long-standing criminological axiom is that impoverished neighborhood conditions lead to an enhanced prevalence of criminality, familial disruption, poor academic performance, and a whole host of other negative social outcomes. A key argument of social-disorganization theorists is that when localities become "unable to provide essential services, such as education, health care, and proper housing . . . they experience significant levels of unemployment, single-parent families, and families on welfare" (Seigel, 2001, p. 191). One way of coping with these deficiencies, social-disorganization theorists argue, is through the utilization of illegal avenues of economic production, such as the drug trade (Byrne & Sampson, 1986). In short, impoverished neighborhoods lack the resources necessary to adequately provide for their residents. Two types of wealth deficiencies have been identified: "social capital" and "human capital."

According to John Hagan, social capital "refers to the social skills and resources needed to effect positive change in neighborhood life" and involves a neighborhood's ability to create "capability through socially structured relations between individuals in groups" (1994, p. 66; Rose & Clear, 1998, 454). Social capital, then, refers to the collective resources available to care for and improve social life in residents' immediate environment. Human capital "refers to the human skill and resources individuals need to function effectively, such as reading, writing, and reasoning ability. Human capital is the capital individuals acquire through education and training for productive purposes" (p. 66).

Socially disorganized communities often have high rates of criminality due to the fact that social and human capital available to residents that might help them succeed through legal avenues is limited in poor neighborhoods. Socially disorganized communities are characterized by isolated groups of individuals who feel they have little connection to the world around them. People are more likely to rent rather than own their homes, more likely to move frequently from residence to residence, and are less likely to form strong ties to their neighbors and community institutions. Moreover, as public resources are diverted toward prisons and away from public programs in education and child care, for example, socially disadvantaged communities struggle all the more. As Dina Rose and Todd Clear argue:

> The macroeconomics of crime policy also damage inner-city communities by shifting government funding priorities away from those communities toward penal institutions. The harsh budgetary politics of the 1990s has corresponded to equally harsh punitive politics in which correctional expenditures have grown by billions of dollars annually while money to support schools, supplement tuition, provide summer jobs for teens, and so forth all received cuts. (1998, p. 462)

Stakeholders in Incarceration

Imprisonment has now long been big business in the United States (Christie, 1993). Layer upon layer of politically or economically vested stakeholders have their interests tied up in the use of imprisonment as punishment for crime (Ericson, McMahon, and Evans, 1993). As a recent study of private prisons in Ohio revealed, state departments of correction have often become the single largest expenditure in state budgets, higher even than spending on public education or health care—with the

Ohio Department of Rehabilitation and Corrections's annual budget, for example, being more than $1 billion (Hallett & Hanauer, 2001). The staggering sums of public money spent on incarceration make capturing even small portions of a state's correctional budget a worthy objective for private vendors. Privatized management and operation of entire prison facilities, however, is only one extreme example of private-sector involvement in prisons. Private-sector connections to both public and private prison systems are widespread, including labor contracts with corporations like IBM, MCI, Motorola, TWA, Victoria's Secret, Compaq computers, and many others (Dyer, 2000, pp. 246–52; Borna, 1986).

In addition to private for-profit corporations using inmate labor, many jurisdictions heavily utilize convict laborers to provide goods and services that would otherwise be obtained via the free market. The state of Florida, for example, has inmate labor involved in quite a diverse set of labor practices including citrus, beef, and dairy production; document reproduction; textiles and clothing; and well-developed office product, optical and eyeglass, and dental industries. Customers eligible to purchase from the prison industry suppliers include state, local, or federal government entities; cities; counties; universities; public schools; foreign government agencies; and not-for-profit businesses. As small businessman and office-product salesman Robert DeGroft told a congressional committee in 2001: "I find it ironic that we have laws in this country that prohibit the US from importing products made by prisoners in other countries, but here at home our own government in many cases is solely dependent on prison labor for its goods" (as cited in Fraser, 2001).

At the federal level, an organization called Federal Prison Industries (FPI), founded during President Franklin Roosevelt's administration in 1934 to provide workforce training and buyers for inmate-produced goods, today has sales of nearly $550 million annually and is ranked thirty-sixth of the one hundred largest federal contractors—being larger than most private vendors doing business with the federal government (Jacoby, 2001). As Jeff Jacoby of the *Boston Globe* recently put it: "FPI has a setup even the Mafia would envy. Both of them make their customers offers they can't refuse. But when FPI does it, it's legal" (ibid.). Jacoby is referring to the mandatory contracting rules that make it illegal for governmental agencies to solicit bids from outside contractors or vendors for goods and services provided by FPI (Fraser, 2001). As the U.S. Chamber of Commerce points out: "Currently, the FPI—a government-owned corporation—has several unfair advantages over 'Main Street' businesses in the federal procurement process: it operates with taxpayer dollars; its workforce earns $1.35 or less per hour; it's exempt from costly safety and health regulations; and it can exercise its special 'mandatory source' status to become the government's sole vendor for a particular product or service, leaving many businesses to scramble for other markets" (2005).

Inmate labor contracts are attractive for many reasons today, and, as Alex Lichtenstein recently suggested, they remain attractive essentially for the same reasons that they were in the mid-1860s (2001). First, of course, one literally has a captive labor force—a guaranteed population of workers available for shift or temporary work on a twenty-four-hour basis. Moreover, inmate labor does not require the expense of benefits such as health care, overtime, sick leave, not to mention paid holidays. During periods of economic expansion or slowdown, furthermore, inmates are readily available to do seasonal or part-time work, without the administrative burden of continuously having to rehire or train a workforce characterized by high turnover. Even when inmates are paid prevailing wages for the work they do, large portions of their earned pay are immediately seized by the state to cover the costs of their confinement (Parenti, 1999). Finally, of course, the need to offer a competitive wage is absent. Inmate labor is attractive to private industry and government in large part because prisoners lack the bargaining power of free labor— enabling private industry to more completely set the terms of employment by offering whatever jobs they choose (Lichtenstein, 1996). Thus, private profit through imprisonment involves not only control of the prisons themselves but also profit-driven schemes within prisons utilizing the captive labor therein. As pointed out by the U.S. Chamber of Commerce—not exactly a leftist organization—this practice arguably compromises free trade and competition and amounts to a government subsidy for the business enterprises involved—also known as "corporate welfare."

Money, Politics, and Zero Accountability for Spending on Imprisonment

Although the for-profit imprisonment industry has not been the cause of what James Austin and John Irwin (2001) call the "imprisonment binge" undertaken over the past twenty years ("tough on crime" politicians seeking reelection were arguably the cause), the industry has certainly been a beneficiary and enabler of it. Whereas conservative "get-tough-on-crime" politicians are often the very same people stridently advocating "no new taxes," increases in spending on prisons have cost the American taxpayers billions. Normally, tax increases are subject to referenda on which the public votes. Not so with private prisons. In fact, private financing of prison construction through corporate-sponsored "lease-payment" bonds that avoid public referenda on tax increases for prison construction has been one of the key selling points of private prisons to legislators throughout the country (Harding, 1997, p. 19; Dyer, 2000, pp. 246–52; Borna, 1986).

Unlike general-revenue bonds, approved by voters and backed by state revenue, lease-payment bonds require higher interest rates and insurance premiums because they are considered "riskier investments" and have not been approved by voters. This is because "most major lease financing is done through a municipal authority—a separate legal entity established by the municipality to issue debt" (Borna, 1986, p. 324). As such, lease-payment bonds do not require competitive bidding and may be approved by public officials without putting the plan in question to voters through a referendum (Bates, 1998; Dyer, 2000, p. 248). Again, several critics of this practice have called it "corporate welfare" (Bates, 1998; Dyer, 2000).

In past arrangements, these monies have been pieced together through corporate backing from Merrill Lynch, Allstate, Sherson Lehman, Smith Barney, and Goldman Sachs and Company (Dyer, 2000, p. 246). One traditional means of public stewardship is voter referenda determining whether new construction for public projects (for instance, schools and prisons) is warranted. In the era of "getting tough on crime" and "no new taxes," however, lease-payment bonds offer politicians a means of acquiring pct projects at public expense while preserving the official pledge to not raise taxes. Even given these outside private financing provisions, of course, taxpayers still ultimately foot the bill for prisons built and operated under lease-payment arrangements.

All of this is to say that in order to understand the politics of prison privatization, one must look deeper than instrumentalist "crime control" objectives. Though nominally devoted to reducing crime, all prisons—and especially for-profit prisons—serve many powerful interests beyond those associated with the crime-fighting agendas often vaunted on their behalf (Garland, 1990; Davis, 1998; Schlosser, 1998). In fact, it may be legal officials and politicians themselves who need prisons most of all—for purposes of electability and generating the popular perception that security is being achieved. The truth, however, is that given the U.S. Department of Justice's official recidivism rate for state prisoners of nearly 70 percent, frankly not much lasting crime control is achieved by incarceration (Langan & Levin, 2002). More fruitful agendas for drug treatment and social rehabilitation have proven more cost-effective and successful with offenders (Harrell et al., 2002; White & Hallett, 2005). Meanwhile, the enormous resources spent on imprisonment go deeper into the pockets of private interests at public expense. As Libertarian privatization proponent Bruce Benson concedes about America's tendency to *overuse* incarceration at the expense of taxpayers regardless of its ineffectiveness:

> Many punishments other than imprisonment are available to judges, and some are frequently employed, but the incentives to consider them are relatively weak because sentencing decisions are made in a political environment in which judges and prosecutors have "free access" to state prison space. Inasmuch as prosecutors and judges have incentives to demonstrate to their local constituencies that they are "tough on crime," imprisonment is a relatively attractive punishment. . . . Thus, all local prosecutors and judges have incentives to choose imprisonment relatively frequently. If there is no quota system in place that forces a judge and prosecutor to limit the flow of criminals into the state prison (e.g. sentencing guidelines determined by the availability of prison capacity rather than by legislators' political goals to appear tough without paying for it), then crowding is inevitable because there is no effective coordination of the sentencing decisions of the dispersed local judges. (1998, p. 135)

Selling For-Profit Imprisonment: There Goes the Neighborhood

> In the course of its routine activities, punishment teaches, clarifies, dramatizes and authoritatively enacts some of the basic moral-political categories and distinctions which help form our symbolic universe. It routinely interprets events, defines conduct, classifies action and evaluates worth, and having done so, it sanctions these judgments with the power and authority of law, forcefully projecting them onto offenders and the public audience alike.
>
> —David Garland, *Punishment and Culture: The Symbolic Dimension of Criminal Justice*

When examining the criminality of ethnic groups in various concentric neighborhood zones of Chicago, Clifford Shaw and Henry McKay (1969) found that criminality is most prevalent in impoverished areas with high rates of transience and deteriorating infrastructure, regardless of race. Ethnic communities not suffering from poverty had much lower rates of crime than impoverished white neighborhoods. As neighborhood and economic development expands from the older center of cities into newer and wealthier suburban outskirts, a process of "invasion, dominance, and succession" takes place in concentric zones surrounding the center. As zones expand away from the inner city, with property values being higher outside the center, transitional neighborhoods ("interstitial areas") "become a battleground between the invading and retreating cultures," suffering higher rates of crime, residential turnover, and citizen disaffection from their neighborhoods and one another in a "siege mentality" (Vold et al., 1998, p. 147). This "ecological" perspective seeks to account for the "interrelationships and interdependencies" between the "physical and economic status" of neighborhoods and their "population compositions" of citizens induced to criminality (pp. 140–157). As Larry Seigel sums it up for many an undergraduate criminology student, Shaw and McKay's research shows that "crime is a constant fixture in areas of poverty regardless of residents' racial or ethnic identity" (2001, p. 193).

An important enhancement to this ecological tradition is recognition of the fact that more recent "criminologies of everyday life" (see Felson, 1994) show how the "routine activities" and behaviors of victims, offenders, and protectors (police and the justice system) contribute dramatically to the social experience of crime (Ericson et al., 1993; see also Garland, 2001a, pp. 103–38). The traditional amelioristic ecological focus on neighborhood deterioration as the prime motivator for criminality, in other words, has now been supplanted by assessments of victim vulnerability (or "target hardening") and availability of capable protectors (more police and jails and prisons), particularly in the most impoverished of neighborhoods. As such, private security forces and for-profit imprisonment venues are used to bolster a weakened public ecosystem, taking the onus of crime control *away* from the police and the state itself and placing it increasingly onto streetwise potential victims, private corporations, and ultimately "markets" (Garland & Sparks, 2000; Garland, 1996, 2001a, p. 128). To the extent these strategies reconstitute society as a contest between consumers, they also heighten the prioritized sense of public vulnerability and reinforce the perceived utility of privatization.

A series of advertisements run by Corrections Corporation of America over the past several years tellingly reveals all three of the above ecological characteristics: a knowing sensitivity to the cogency of "place" as a representation of security and stability, attributions to the ineffectiveness of the state "monopoly" on crime control, and faithful adherence to the notion that the capitalistic market system will order social life in healthy (and moral) ways. The CCA advertisements presented below also strategically feature minorities in suburban neighborhoods or contexts, with minority CCA employees as representatives and protectors of them.

Several recent CCA advertisements feature minority employees and a fourth with an African American first grader under this heading: "Would You Rather Spend $11 More a Day on a Convicted Criminal or an Inspired First Grader?" (Figure 3.1). By presenting private prisons in this way, of course, the state is relieved of its responsibility to reduce crime through rehabilitation, while offenders are rendered punishable commodities worthy of utilization in a market system (where crime reduction is a worthy for-profit rather than curative enterprise) (see Garland, 2001a). The pigtailed schoolgirl portrayed in the ad is explicitly reminiscent of Norman Rockwell's famous portrait of school desegregation, *The Problem We All Live With: Schoolgirl with U.S. Marshals* (see Buechner, 1972) and of Rockwell's other pictorials of racial desegregation of America's public schools as well as racial integration of the white suburbs (Figures 3.2, 3.3) (Coles, 2000; Buechner, 1972, pp. 136–37; Finch, 1975, pp. 209–10).

In another ad, an African American woman is depicted as a teacher at a chalkboard, ostensibly teaching CCA inmates in a CCA classroom. Clearly visible on the blackboard in the CCA ad are the terms *socialization, stratification,* and *family. Socialization* is defined as "the process by which an individual learns the customs of his or her society" (Figure 3.4). Not surprisingly, the definition of *stratification* provided on the board in the CCA ad below is not one involving capitalistic exploitation of incarcerated masses, but "the division of society into various classes based on income, education, and values." Finally, *family* is defined as "a family . . . of a mother." Conspicuously missing from this phrase are the words *and father*—obscured by the teacher standing at the board? Above the teacher in the text of the ad are the words EDUCATION, COUNSELING, RELIGION in large block letters, perhaps foretelling the next moralistic wave of prison privatization, the so-called faith-based prisons movement (Hallett, 2002a). Nearby prisons run by corporations are thus not portrayed as a threat to neighborhood stability, but rather exist as strongholds in service of "well-socialized" (and baldly stratified) neighborhood protection.

Figure 3.1 CCA's "First Grader" advertisement.

Figure 3.2 The Problem We All Live With. Copyright 1964 The Norman Rockwell Family Trust. Reproduced by permission of the Norman Rockwell Estate Licensing Company, Niles, Ill.

Figure 3.3 Moving Day, also known as *New Kids in the Neighborhood.* Copyright 1967 The Norman Rockwell Family Trust. Reproduced by permission of the Norman Rockwell Estate Licensing Company, Niles, Ill.

EDUCATION. COUNSELING. RELIGION.

VOCATIONAL TRAINING. DRUG TREATMENT.

JUST ANOTHER DAY

AT A CCA PRISON.

A day at a Corrections Corporation of America prison is not what you might think. In addition to operating facilities that are modern, tightly managed and highly secure, we also challenge inmates with a range of programs designed to make their time more productive. Our educational, counseling, recreational, vocational training and substance abuse treatment programs help give CCA inmates a chance to turn their lives around. In fact, our substance abuse treatment program is recognized around the world. We provide these programs in partnership with government because we believe it makes a difference in inmate rehabilitation and in public safety. To learn more about CCA, contact James H. Ball, Vice President, Business Development, at 615-263-3000 or jamesball@correctionscorp.com.

CCA
CORRECTIONS CORPORATION OF AMERICA

QUIETLY GOING ABOUT THE BUSINESS OF PUBLIC SAFETY.

Figure 3.4 CCA's "Schooldays" advertisement.

In another ad, a Hispanic man (Hispanics being the second most populace minority group in CCA prisons) stands with a little boy on his bike, baseball glove visible, the man wearing a CCA baseball cap in a white-picket-fenced neighborhood, a presumptive middle-class CCA employee (Figure 3.5).[1] Another interesting thing about these ads, however, is that they began to appear in the immediate aftermath of several high-profile escapes from CCA facilities in Tennessee and around the country (see Chapter 4).

In yet another ad, an African American employee, this time a CCA guard, is depicted with the CCA moniker featured prominently on his arm as he speaks watchfully into a patrol radio (Figure 3.6). As noted prison privatization scholar David Shichor explains:

> Having a private corporation's badge on the correctional officer's uniform sends socially meaningful signals. . . . [I]t confirms that in a capitalist society profit making is an almost "sacred" principle and that it is a good and acceptable business practice to make money by entrepreneurs and investors (having surplus money to invest) on the legal infliction of pain and suffering (what punishment amounts to) on inmates, who by and large come from the lower socio-economic segments of society. (1998, pp. 93–94)

In short, these advertisements extolling the virtues of for-profit prisons emphasize their role in maintaining neighborhood stability and safety and feature CCA employees as both exemplars and protectors of that ecological order. Put another way, the continued overincarceration of mostly nonviolent minority offenders by a for-profit corporation is justified here in traditional value-laden terms: "family," "values," "religion," and "customs." Alas, the criminological argument of the drug war: in order to reduce crime, society itself is not what needs changing, it is the itinerant criminal in the custody of the well-meaning corporation needing "socialization," that they might accept the "stratified" order and be instilled with "religion" and "family" values. As Austin Turk puts it:

> Traditional criminology assumes that the person is the problem, so the objective is to explain what is wrong with the person that makes him or her do bad things. This fits well the common assumption that interpersonal relations and individual behavior are somehow more "real" than social structure and organizational behavior. Moreover, it satisfies the political preference for "safe problem definitions, explanations, and solu-

Figure 3.5 CCA's "Bike and Ball Glove" advertisement.

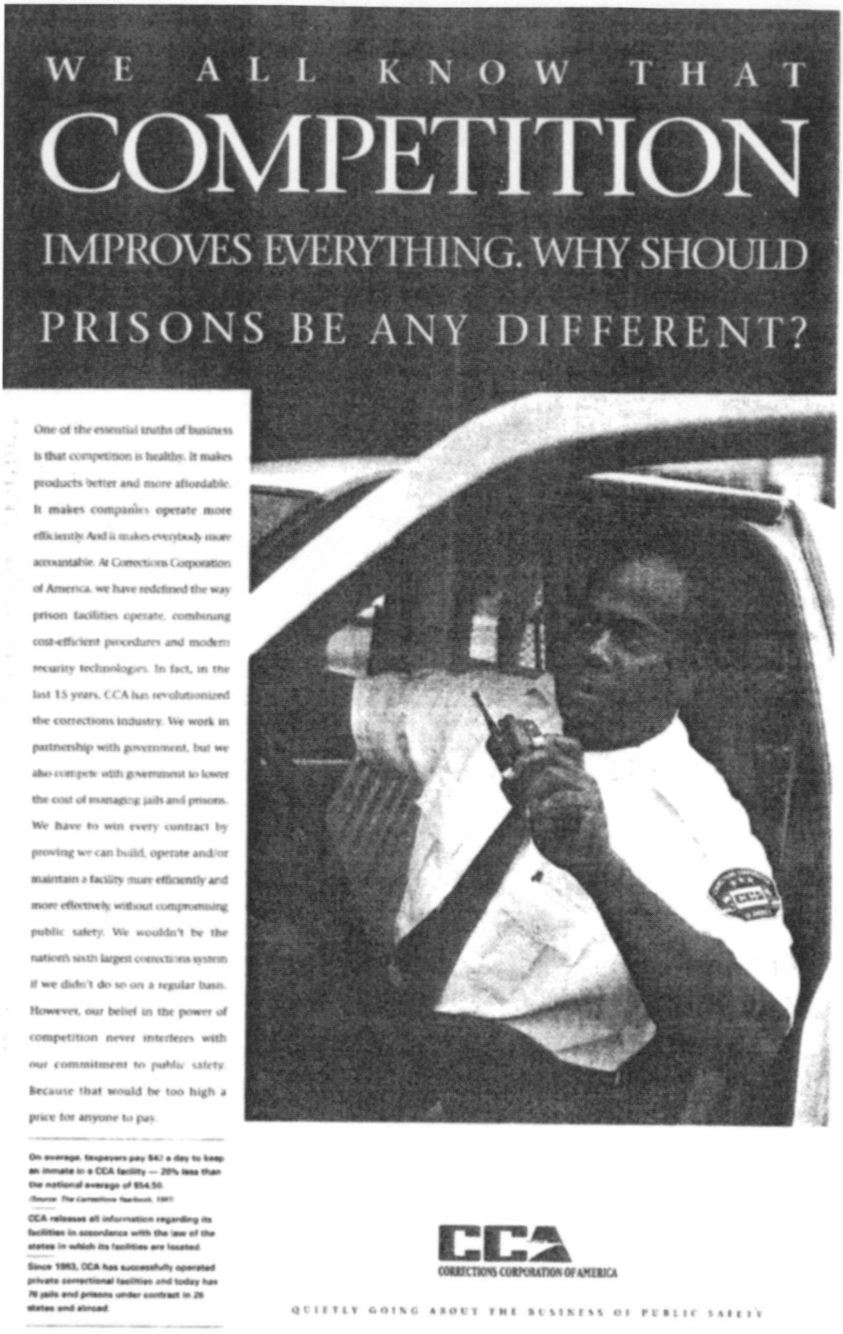

Figure 3.6 CCA's "Guard" advertisement.

tions—that is, those that do not question the way in which society is organized. (1995, p. 15)

These advertisements, of course, belie the fact that the solid majority of inmates in CCA's prisons both nationwide and in Tennessee (where the ads first appeared) are racial minorities from disadvantaged backgrounds (TNDOC, 1998, pp. 55, 77; Bureau of Justice Statistics, 1999). In short, CCA sells itself by purporting to protect (and represent) a middle-class ecology by incarcerating people largely excluded from it. Drawing from his research on the ghetto as "an instrument of control and confinement," Loïc Wacquant further suggests: "One can even hypothesize that . . . there is every chance that the societies of Western Europe will generate analogous, albeit less pronounced, situations to the extent that they, too, embark on the path of the penal management of poverty and inequality, and ask their prison system not only to curb crime but also to regulate the lower segments of the labor market and to hold at bay populations judged to be disreputable, derelict, and unwanted" (1999, p. 216).

Conclusion: Social Disorganization as Market Opportunity

This country is on the verge of a social catastrophe because of the sheer number of African-Americans behind bars—numbers that continue to rise with breathtaking speed and frightening implications. The reason: our criminal justice policies are preventing many African Americans from claiming their stake in the American dream, thereby contributing to the destruction of our national ideal of racial harmony.

—Steven Donziger, *The Real War on Crime*

A 1997 Prudential-Securities analysis of the for-profit prison industry identified four key threats to its long-term viability: falling crime, shorter prison terms, alternatives to incarceration, and reductions in the use of mandatory prison sentences for nonviolent drug crime (Schlosser, 1998). The public, of course—unlike the private prison industry—has a certain direct interest in falling crime, with fewer offenders resulting in fewer victims and less need to incarcerate. Society has a criminological and financial interest as well in maintaining its capacity to offer a wide range of *non*incarcerative punishments for nonviolent criminals. As Joan Petersilia, past president of the American Society of Criminology, puts it: "Drug clinics do more to rehabilitate drug addicts than prison; job training does more to reduce recidivism than jails; and early childhood prevention programs do more than any other factor to reduce a propensity to crime" (1994, p. 176). Excessive spending on incarceration, as the ever more conventional punishment for even nonviolent crime, drains resources from other sanctioning options with lower overall costs and greater long-term effectiveness.

As David Garland argues in an important article titled "Punishment and Culture: The Symbolic Dimension of Criminal Justice": "Nowadays 'the prison' is as much a basic metaphor of our cultural imagination as it is a feature of our penal policy" (1991, p. 203). From the perspective of social-disorganization theory, privatization as a solution to overcrowded and costly prisons leaves the ecological sources of crime unaddressed and, in this case, the fountain of all profits—large populations of disfranchised surplus population trapped in the inner city to be incarcerated for nonviolent drug crime—conveniently intact (Irwin & Austin, 1996; Wilson, 1996). By drawing on "Rockwellian" iconography, CCA seeks to exploit canonized mercantile depictions of the American dream supportive of the expanded use of for-profit prisons—but by and on behalf of people more typically excluded from it. As Jan Cohn notes in a book on the *Saturday Evening Post* titled *Creating America: George Horace Lorimer and the Saturday Evening Post*, for which Rockwell was the premier illustrator, this is not surprising:

> The *Post* was conceived by both [George Horace] Lorimer and [Cyrus H.] Curtis as the medium of an American consciousness. Geographically, as a national magazine, it was intended to transcend local markets dominated by newspapers. Intellectually, as a general-interest magazine printing both fiction and non-fiction on a wide variety of subjects, it was designed to reach audiences ignored by "highbrow" magazines like *Harper's* and the *Atlantic*. Commercially, as a magazine that carried national advertising and allied itself with the newest business economics of standardization and national distribution, the *Post* was created to echo and reinforce in its contents the emerging concept of America as a nation unified by consumption of standardized commodities. (1989, p. 9; emphasis added)

In today's era of globalization and devolution, the antagonisms associated with social inequality mildly held in check by governmental commitment to social welfare have been displaced by far more limited agendas seeking to *profitably* mitigate the symptoms of society's underlying illnesses. The renewed multinational character of today's for-profit imprisonment industry raises the specter of the return to a transnational system of commerce in dispossessed human beings eerily reminiscent of transportation, just as new affirmations of retrenchment and abandonment of the welfare state come loudly from affluent suburbs.

FOUR

Money and Power: The Political Economy of Prison Privatization

The prison industrial complex is not only a set of interest groups and institutions. It is also a state of mind.

—Eric Schlosser, "The Prison Industrial Complex"

"A State of Mind": Punishment as Culturally Revealing

Since Enlightenment-era thinkers began to conceptualize prison as a tool for engineering lower crime rates, prisons have played a central role in the public mind regarding criminality. Correctional philosophies have changed radically over time, evolving to reflect changing political, religious, and legal sensibilities. Whether through "rehabilitation," "incapacitation," "deterrence," or "retribution," prison administrators have implemented varying regimens of penalty according to changes in prevailing thinking about social control. Approaches to punishment, therefore, should always be understood as fluid and evolving over time according to prevailing interests, sensibilities, and values.

The philosophies and justifications for

the use of imprisonment have also undergone dramatic transformation. When viewed historically, the changing rationales and philosophies justifying imprisonment reveal that there is much more going on in the social act of punishment than just "crime control." Put simply, prisons and what goes on in them are contemporaneous expressions of the broader culture.

A well-established tradition of viewing punishment as serving agendas *other* than crime control has long existed in criminology—including the work of Emile Durkheim (1933), who argues that punishment is more directed at the audience than the offender and enhances social solidarity; George Herbert Mead (1918), who asserts that punishment releases inhibited social aggression; Georg Rusche and Otto Kirchheimer (1968), who contend that incarceration rates fluctuate with labor and economic demand; Michel Foucault (1977), who views punishment strategies as part of a larger "modern" disciplinary strategy of social control; and David Garland (1990), who sees punishments as cultural expressions involving complex economic, moral, political, as well as functional aims. Many great social scientists have argued that understanding imprisonment as a social institution requires exploring the social purposes it may be serving *other* than crime control. As David Garland puts it: "In designing penal policy we are not simply deciding how to deal with a group of people on the margins of society—whether to deter, reform, or incapacitate them and if so how. Nor are we simply deploying power or economic resources for penological ends. We are also and at the same time defining ourselves and our society in ways which may be quite central to our cultural and political identity" (1990, 276).

Asking Questions about Punishment

As noted above, prisons have become socially accepted symbols of crime control in American society. A vast number of stakeholders with life sustaining ties to the practice of imprisonment make prisons complex social institutions (that is, labor unions, consumers, politicians, voters, communities seeking tax-base stability, university researchers, citizens hungry for jobs, private manufacturing and information technology firms, lobbyists, academics, and, not least, prisoners and their families). What kinds of things are "accomplished" by prisons other than crime control? What political interests are served by expanding imprisonment even in the face of evidence that prisons largely fail to control crime?

Prisons give people jobs, provide labor for high-tech production and information technology firms, increase a jurisdiction's population for census counts, enhance tax-base stability, and above all convince people that "something is being done" about crime (Liebling, 2004; Chambliss, 2001). Many people's lives and livelihoods are also tied to the continuous expansion of incarceration as a social policy. These livelihoods are well represented by interest groups, such as correctional officers' employee unions, victims' rights groups, private corporations, and get-tough-on-crime politicians. If prisons are used disproportionately against one particular group, this is also socially meaningful, not just in terms of an obvious power imbalance between groups but also for what it says about the culture itself.

Certainly it is true that the crimes of the lower classes have been more heavily policed and punished than those of the wealthy in the United States throughout its history (Shelden, 2001; Chambliss, 2001). When the lion's share of criminal justice resources are used to fight only narrowly defined types of crime, however, then the prison system arguably plays a de facto role, not of reducing criminality through rehabilitation or punishment, but of reordering social life along lines of preexisting power.

Although many people view imprisonment as justly deserved "revenge" exacted upon offenders for breaking the social contract—arguing that imprisonment is justified regardless of incarceration's crime-control utility—this contrasts profoundly with the dominant "correctional" philosophy prevalent since the "birth of the prison," which has emphasized rehabilitation and "reform" of the offender (Parenti, 1999, pp. 163–69; Pepinsky, 2002; Garland, 2001a; Foucault, 1977). The dominant motif of imprisonment in American history, in fact, rests on the "correctional" capacity of the prison experience. The perfectibility of man has always been an underlying assumption of the process of corrections, until recently. Today, however, a "custodial" philosophy dominates (especially private) prisons. Here, the emphasis is on getting through the day—serving meals, maintaining security, and managing the inmate count as cheaply as possible—rather than rehabilitation, retraining, or reform of offenders (Austin & Irwin, 2001).

Shell Game: Public Money, Private Interests

To really understand America's incarceration binge and criminal justice crackdown, we need to move from an interest-group-based model to a more holistic class analysis that looks at the needs of the class system and class society in general.

—Christian Parenti, *Lockdown America: Police and Prisons in the Age of Crisis*

Today's condition of mass imprisonment of African American men is driven by several forces operating in unison: growing fear of crime, middle-class downward mobility and anger about diminishing security, and increasing political reluctance to view government as responsible for fixing social problems. As mentioned in Chapter 1, David Garland refers to this collection of forces as "the crime complex" (2001a). Profit making through custodial (rather than rehabilitative) imprisonment is today seen by many as both good policy and "good business." The political economy of prison privatization thus has two highly visible features that obscure the more complex social forces driving it: the "law and order" appeal of imprisonment as a response to crime and a matched-up conservative political ideology emphasizing "personal responsibility" over macrolevel changes in society, industry, and employment (Ryan & Ward, 1989).

Under the headings of "devolution" and "federalism," this agenda expands privately controlled, as opposed to public or governmentally controlled, mechanisms of social regulation and welfare. In this literally "new world order," capitalistic markets are increasingly promoted as the most moral, efficient, and appropriate arbiter of social life (Shichor, 1995; Ryan & Ward, 1989). The irony, of course, is that the vast majority of private "alternatives" to governmental programs *are still financed through public taxpayer monies*—and in that sense are still "government" programs. As documented in the next section of this chapter, the subgovernmental network of interests delivering public monies into private hands remains largely unregulated. Recent revelations about "no bid contracts" and "sweetheart deals" from the government to the private sector should give pause about privatization's actual utility for taxpayers (Parenti, 1999). These issues aside, however, it would be a dramatic oversimplification to believe that prison privatization is simply the result of a change in *correctional* philosophy.

From the perspective of critical criminology, "getting tough on crime," "devolving" governmental responsibility for establishing and protecting social welfare, and stressing limited use of government resources for social welfare are symptoms of broader economic and political movements under way in society and the world. *Thus, private prisons fit into a larger matrix of social change, being nominally tied to the agenda of crime control but also serving many other political purposes and private interests.* This "devolutionary" market-driven/"privatization" is also widespread beyond crime and punishment, affecting other areas of social policy making as well, including education, health care, social security, child welfare, and airport security. ₁

The Perfect Storm: "Terror," Devolution, and Fear of Crime

In speaking about the "military industrial complex," political scientist Robert Sherrill notes that the military buildup of the Eisenhower era was propped up by a rather vague but powerful fear of foreign "enemies." Public ignorance of foreign affairs, claims of an American "missile gap" with the Soviets (subsequently disproved), and the much touted fear that the United States was "falling behind" led politicians to characterize expanded military spending as an issue of national survival (Sherrill, 1984; Reeves, 1993). In much the same way, in 1989, President George H. W. Bush touted the war on drugs as the leading problem in America and an issue of "national security." In both the cold war and the drug war, "suitable enemies" figured prominently (Wacquant, 1999). Needless to say, the continuous drumbeat of the "war on terror" also relies heavily on the identification of a seemingly nebulous set of potentially omnipresent enemies that has already arguably confused illegal Mexican laborers with Arab foreign infiltrators (Welch, 2005).

To gain popular support for "getting tough on crime," U.S. politicians of both major political parties have successfully employed a highly racialized strategy of associating public disorder with minority groups, rather than with macrolevel shifts in economic well-being or opportunity (Beckett & Sasson, 2000b; Clear, 1997; Parenti, 1999; Wilson, 1996, 1999; Greenberg & West, 2001). These moral entrepreneurs shifted public resources away from ameliorative and preventative social programs and directed them, instead, toward crime control and the building of a "security state"—an agenda well under way before September 11, 2001 (Beckett & Sasson, 2000b; Welch, 2005).

The welfare state was undermined, in particular, by a racialized change in the moral status of the poor from "deserving" to "undeserving." According to Katherine Beckett and Theodore Sasson: "This transformation of the moral status of the poor was predicated on a change in the identity of the prototypical poor person from white and rural (in the imagery of the Great Depression and the war on poverty) to black and urban (in the iconography of the wars on crime and drugs)" (2000b, p. 68). Thus, although criminal justice is still primarily a local enterprise, there is a powerful similarity between the central role the federal government has played in both the "war on crime" and the cold war. Starting especially with Barry Goldwater in 1964—a hawkish cold warrior—and later with the administration of Richard Nixon, conservative political activists recognized the value of "the crime problem" as a vehicle for winning votes, particularly from alienated southern white Democrats (Beckett, 1997; Epstein, 1977; Parenti, 1999). "Federalizing" crime policy became a viable political strategy.

Coming out of the turbulent 1960s, policy changes revealing the success of this strategy, such as those put forward in the Omnibus Crime Control and Safe Streets Act of 1968, were already apparent. "At the heart of this new type of politics was a very old political trope: Crime meant urban, urban meant black, and the war on crime meant a bulwark built against the increasingly political and vocal racial 'other' by the predominantly white state" (Parenti, 1999, p. 7).

In the process of orchestrating the war on crime, conservative activists successfully had to recharacterize crime control from being a primarily local and preventative enterprise to one necessitating federal government involvement in a "war" against individual offenders deserving of punishment. By the late 1980s, "the debate about crime was galvanized into camps—the liberals and conservatives. Was a person in favor of the criminal or the victim? Did someone believe in rehabilitation or punishment?" (Clear, 1997, p. 139). *Crime, in other words, became a moral issue, much more so than one of policy design, economy, or law.* In this context, punishment soon became the dominant and most frequently prescribed solution, even by otherwise "liberal" politicians. This was not a top-down conspiracy as much as a broader cultural shift involving economics, demographic and media sensibilities, and preexisting racial tensions.

Whereas poverty and "public order" discussions of the past focused on jobs, employment training, and worker placement, the new paradigm focused on implementing wider use of punishment and reducing the size of government (Tonry & Petersilia, 2000; Wilson, 1996, 1999). Indeed, by the presidency of Ronald Reagan, some politicians were promoting "mandatory sentencing" as the greatest means of improving life in poor communities (Clear, 1997). By the 1990s, the conservative paradigm for crime and punishment was so firmly in place that incarceration rates increased *faster* during the presidency of Democrat Bill Clinton than during that of either conservative Republican Reagan or George H. W. Bush (Justice Policy Institute, 2002).

The harshness and corresponding ineffectiveness of our punishment schemes raise our earlier question about crime control. When we declare "wars" on crime, do we do so against corrupt accounting firms that cost thousands of jobs and hundreds of millions of dollars, such as in the recent Enron and WorldCom scandals, or do we declare war against the poor, relatively defenseless, uneducated, and *already largely helpless* "street offender"? Why is this so? Why don't we fight all crime equally? As criminologist Joan Petersilia recently stated in a New York Times editorial: "This data shows unequivocally that get-tough-on-crime laws haven't worked. In fact, recidivism rates (as measured by new arrests) are actually higher a decade after 'getting tough' than they were in the 1980s when we were supposedly so 'lenient'" (Butterfield, 2002). Meanwhile, the incarceration rate increases, fueled by a continuous influx of economically and politically dispossessed prisoners. A recent story in the periodical *Investors Business Daily* analyzing the private prison industry, suggesting "good times might be coming," cites increasingly high recidivism as a source of future private prison revenue. As Cornell Corrections president Steve Logan recently stated in the same story: "Statistics suggest that two-thirds of released prisoners will become repeat offenders and end up back in a cell. Cornell can keep turning a profit while working to counter that trend" (Elliott, 2002). In the aftermath of September 11, for-profit imprisonment is all the more viable, but it was already on the rise before 9/11 (Welch, 2005).

Playing the Race Card: The Political Expedience of Crime Control

Disregarding evidence that the levels of drug use were already in decline, that drug use is not responsive to criminal penalties, that criminalization brings its own pathologies (notably street violence and disrespect for authorities), and that declaring a war against drugs is, in effect, to declare a war against minorities, the US government proceeded to declare such a war and to persist in pursuing it, despite every indication of its failure. Why? Because the groups most adversely

affected lack political power and are widely regarded as dangerous
and undeserving; because the groups least affected could be assured
that something is being done and lawlessness is not tolerated; and
because few politicians are willing to oppose a policy when there is so
little political advantage to be gained by doing so.

   —David Garland, *The Culture of Control: Crime and Social Order in
   Contemporary Society*

As discussed in Chapter 1, the disproportionate impact of the war on
drugs has been in the African American community. By failing to target
a full range of drugs used by a full range of people (whites and blacks),
the drug war "targeted" drugs used primarily by blacks (Lauritsen &
Sampson, 1998, p. 63; Mauer, 2000; Tonry, 1995; Miller, 1996). Drug
laws, in fact, have long proven to be effective tools for controlling what
Randall Shelden calls the "dangerous classes" (2001). Many drugs such as
cocaine and opium were freely used in the United States through the late
1880s, not to mention alcohol and tobacco. As immigration of Chinese,
Irish, Italian, and other foreigners expanded in the United States near the
turn of the century, attitudes and laws regarding specific drugs and their
proper use began to change (Gusfield, 1963). As the drug-using habits of
newcomers to America became more influential in the dominant culture,
particular ideologies about "proper" drug use began to emerge specific
to various groups using various drugs.

   According to Shelden, "Myths about the invincibility of 'crazed'
African Americans under the influence of cocaine were created and perpetuated through newspaper headlines such as one in 1913, which read:
'Drug Crazed Negroes Fire at Every One in Sight in Mississippi Town'"
(2001, pp. 49–50). In short, the history of drug regulation is one of hyp-
ocritical enforcement patterns, targeting only select groups of people
and the drugs they use rather than drug use in general (Gusfield, 1963;
Shelden, 2001, pp. 49–53). Racial tensions and drug-related punishment
schemes have a long history in the United States (Gusfield, 1963).

Fear of Crime: Good to the Last Drop

As David Greenberg and Valerie West argue, "Sociological analyses of the
history of penality have taken as their premise that institutionalized punishment practices are not entirely determined by the functional necessity
of preventing crimes" (2001, p. 638). Instead, diverse agendas involving
cultural and expressive goals such as retribution and revenge, fear of

increasingly powerful "others," shifts in labor market practices, or popular sensibility about basic "human rights" have all been used to explain developments in punishment schemes (Rusche & Kirchheimer, 1968; Elias, 1978, 1982; Foucault, 1977; Mead, 1918; Gusfield, 1963; Garland, 1990). From this perspective, rather than reducing crime, modes of punishment and penalty are products of preexisting structures and thereby work to reconstitute already existing power relationships. "The multi-level operations of power within social practices" complicate efforts to understand imprisonment—but, as noted above, they must be considered in order to comprehensively understand the full range of imprisonment's social functions (C. West, 1999, p. 279).

A well-documented awareness among politicians regarding the political dividends of fighting crime has brought about very dramatic shifts in imprisonment policy over the past twenty-five years (Beckett, 1997; Clear, 1997; Parenti, 1999; Tonry, 1995; Mauer, 2000). In terms of the drug war, differential sanctions for whites versus blacks in their use of drugs have been well documented. The Anti–Drug Abuse Act of 1986 implemented harsh punishments specifically for crack cocaine (used primarily by blacks) and lesser punishments for the powdered form of cocaine (used primarily by whites). Smaller amounts of crack were legislated harsher punishments than larger amounts of its powder form by "100 to 1" (Shelden, 2001, p. 59). "Under federal law, possession of five grams of crack cocaine became a felony that carried a *mandatory minimum* sentence of five years, while possession of the same amount of powder cocaine remained a misdemeanor punishable by a *maximum* of one year (Donziger, 1996, p. 118). *The Anti–Drug Abuse Act "made crack cocaine the only drug under the act with a mandatory minimum penalty for a first offense of simple possession"* (Shelden, 2001, p. 60; emphasis added).

Although the purported rationale for this dramatic disparity in sentencing between whites and blacks was that "crack causes violence," much of the violence associated with crack cocaine was arguably *caused* by law enforcement itself, as inner-city drug sellers fought to overcome the temporary market displacement brought about by the drug war. "In the process of that displacement, violence erupted as dealers jockeyed to control market share" (Donziger, 1996, p. 119; see also Goldstein, Brownstein, Ryan, & Bellucci, 1997; and Baumer, 1994).

According to the sociological tradition for understanding punishment, a plausible explanation for the sentencing disparity between whites and blacks in the drug war is *race*. As Greenberg and West recently stated (borrowing a phrase from Jerome Skolnick [1966]): "Blacks—black males in particular—appear to have become 'symbolic assailants' whose presence in a city evokes fear of crime independently of their actual level of crime" (2001, p. 640). Though self-report data consistently indicate that both whites and blacks use drugs at similar (and fairly high) rates, the "targeting" of drug use in the inner city by law enforcement at least partially accounts for the massive disparity in incarceration for drug crime (Donziger, 1995, p. 115; Lauritsen & Sampson, 1998, p. 76; Tonry, 1995). "Police found more drugs in minority communities, because that's where they looked for them. Had they pointed the drug war at college campuses, it is likely that our jails would now be filled overwhelmingly with university students" (Donziger, 1995, p. 115).

Of course, orchestrating a drug war against largely white middle-class students on college campuses (whose parents can afford attorneys) is a vastly different social enterprise than combating drug use in the inner city. Politically and economically weak residents of inner cities pose little risk for backlash, whereas moralistic crackdowns on the drug-using habits of "others" have proven a winning staple of American electoral politics since the late 1800s, as noted above (Shelden, 2001). Thus, orchestrating public fear of drug-crazed "others" dangerous to the body politic has long suited the interests of politicians and perhaps those especially who have strenuously promoted our various "wars" on drugs.

The Military Industrial Complex versus the Crime Control Complex

Thus, the "crime complex" mentioned in Chapter 1, so instrumental in keeping crime and punishment a central budgetary, political, and cultural issue, to this point has been more heavily driven by *local* stakeholders than was the "military industrial complex" of which President Eisenhower warned. The broad array of political and economic interests served by imprisonment extends beyond those of a powerful elite exerting undue influence over the expansion of military budgets (Parenti, 1999; Lilly & Knepper, 1993). It is a truism, however, that the commerce surrounding both correctional and military expenditures is massive. In fact, it is not uncommon in recent years to find states such as California and Ohio in which the single largest item in the state budget *is* the prison system for several years running (Hallett & Hanauer, 2001).

Finally, it is important to emphasize that although the events of September 11, 2001, may have expanded the available population of "suitable enemies" worthy of incarceration, the practice of mass incarceration of the marginal was already well under way before then (Wacquant, 1999). The profit motive itself has been more than enough incentive for expanding the crime complex years prior to 9/11 (see Hallinan, 2001). "Suitable enemies" both foreign and domestic fall easy prey to the entrepreneurial agendas of American and international capitalists (Wacquant, 1999).

With all of the cautions noted, there is certainly one very ominous similarity between the "military industrial complex" and the "crime complex": the federal government's recent trend toward offering financial incentives for prison construction, such as in the 1994 Violent Crime Control and Law Enforcement Act. This accounts for the largest share of the increase in federal criminal justice spending prior to September 11, 2001. One should also note that whereas federal spending on criminal justice ranks lower than state, local, or municipal spending, it also saw the largest percentage increase since the early 1980s. This increase demonstrates an increasing presence of the federal government in what was previously the almost exclusively localized enterprise of criminal justice (Greenberg & West, 2001). Although state and especially local agencies are the criminal justice system's feeder source for prisoners, these jurisdictions have little disincentive for avoiding imprisonment—and, indeed, sometimes through privatization have a direct economic incentive to expand it at virtually no cost to themselves.

Taking the Devil's Bargain: Capitalist Ecology and Crime Control

Communities today find themselves increasingly beholden to corporate interests demanding large tax concessions for the privilege of locating in job-hungry jurisdictions. In order to lure businesses into communities, many local leaders "give away the farm," so to speak, by granting tax exemptions and reduced levies on construction and other fees. Community leaders do so because they fully recognize their constituents' dependency on corporate wealth for tax-base stability and basic incomes. Decades of research on crime indicate a direct link between available economic resources in communities and the development of the kinds of social and human capital that inhibits criminality (Sampson & Wilson,

2000). The private prison industry is no exception to this rule, with the promise of jobs eventually overcoming citizens' aversion to locating prisons "in the backyards" of residents. All tax concessions given up by communities to private prison firms, of course, have to be factored in as "hidden costs" of the venture—and as more resources are spent on incarceration, fewer resources are available for other social priorities.

In cases from Youngstown, Ohio, to Thomson, Illinois, to Stanley, Wisconsin, to Greenwood, Mississippi, communities have been making devil's bargains with prison firms, in hopes of securing jobs in their economically depressed communities (Harden, 2002; Marcott, 2002; Chaptman, 2002). In Youngstown, for example, the city's Board of Education filed suit against the city and Corrections Corporation of America "over tax breaks the city granted the private prison company. The dispute dates to 1994, when a new state law required that cities get the approval of school boards before handing out tax breaks of more than 75 percent. But the city wanted to continue giving out 100 percent tax incentives to attract new businesses to town. . . . If the city loses, CCA wants the city to pay anything the company may owe to the school district." Mayor George McKelvey's reply to this request: "That would bankrupt the city of Youngstown" (Smith & Cole, 2002).

As documented in Chapter 3, clear differences exist between neighborhoods in levels of crime and social disorganization. The "civilized" world is divided into good neighborhoods and bad, with people wanting *into* the former and *out* of the latter. Without question, the ecologies of some neighborhoods offer more access to human and social capital than others: good schools, access to social services, and environments not filled with violence (Sampson & Raudenbush, 2001). At the same time, it is not uncommon today to find jurisdictions spending less on education and devoting fewer resources to social programming while devoting more resources for "security." This focus on security, however, shifts attention away from nurturing the future of upcoming generations in favor of protecting the interests of select pockets of the current generation. Good neighborhoods become more irrevocably the province of the "haves." At the same time, the population of those having access to neighborhood ecologies that nurture and protect, shrinks (Freeman, 2001).

In order to attract businesses, however, city leaders often feel pressure to cut taxes, thereby undermining already existing needs—and future potential for improvement. Whereas a key facet of a sound social ecology is adequate economic viability, communities desperate enough will compromise their futures in order to make economic ends meet in the present. The Youngstown lawsuit mentioned above, for example, hinged on the city's leveraging money for prison construction that would otherwise have gone to the school board for education. *As these resources are cut, already marginalized public systems of service suffer the disproportionate brunt of the loss in the name of sustaining private profitability.* With for-profit imprisonment, the most vicious of cycles is created. As one Youngstown resident put it to me: "We are now eating our young."

Criminal Justice "Subgovernments"

To deliver up bodies destined for profitable punishment, the political economy of prisons relies on racialized assumptions of criminality—such as images of black welfare mothers reproducing criminal children—and on racist practices in arrest, conviction, and sentencing patterns. Colored bodies constitute the main human raw material in this vast experiment to disappear the major social problems of our time. The prison industrial system materially and morally impoverishes its inhabitants and devours the social wealth needed to address the very problems that have led to spiraling numbers of prisoners.

—Angela Davis, "Reflections on the Prison Industrial Complex"

So how do initiatives to privatize prison systems actually take place? What evidence of "other forces" (economic, political, capitalistic) driving imprisonment is available? The second half of this chapter offers a case study from the state of Tennessee, the home state of Corrections Corporation of America, and the site of the largest-ever prison privatization initiative. As noted in Chapter 1, I was involved as a consultant to a labor union fighting the proposal to privatize Tennessee's prisons at the time it was under consideration.

As already discussed, for-profit imprisonment schemes remove a traditional disincentive for massive spending (on incarceration) by making high crime rates *profitable*. Oftentimes, economically depressed jurisdictions like Youngstown encourage and even solicit for-profit prison firms to build large prisons in their communities. These cities will often, as in the case of Youngstown, waive property-taxes and provide other incentives, even at the expense of local public schools, with the hope of generating business where none exists. Often referred to as the "prison industrial complex," a loose network of political, economic, and legal stakeholders frequently enables the establishment and expansion of for-profit imprisonment through the formation of a "subgovernment" (Palumbo, 1986).[1] Acting collectively in a cooperative fashion, subgovernments constitute unelected and largely unaccountable networks operating toward specific agendas. These subgovernmental networks tend to strengthen over time and to become central stakeholders within their sphere of influence. Speaking directly about prison privatization, J. Robert Lilly & Paul Knepper outline the key elements of a prison privatization subgovernment:

> 1) The participants in a subgovernment share a close working relationship; 2) Close ties between industry and government are reinforced by a steady flow of personnel; 3) subgovernments operate with a low level of visibility and a high degree of effectiveness from the point of view of those inside the subgovernment; 4) subgovernments have a tendency to become fixtures within a given policy arena. (1993, pp. 153–54)

Below is a detailed case study of a privatization subgovernment operative in the state of Tennessee, home state of the world's largest for-profit corrections firm, Corrections Corporation of America. The next portion of this chapter documents the interconnections of this subgovernment and CCA's bid to take over the entire Tennessee prison system in 1997–1998.

Although privatization subgovernments without question have had tremendous influence on the development and expansion of for-profit imprisonment, as will be documented in exacting detail below in the case of Tennessee, it is also important to reiterate that most prisoners are sent to state prisons and local jails by state and local officials "with different agendas, constituencies, incentives, and constraints" than the policy elites of any subgovernment (Greenberg & West, 2001, p. 618). The fiscal interests of local court systems, for example, are not directly served by the large numbers of people they send to state prison, nor are police budgets directly impacted by incarceration rates (Benson, 1998). Broader shifts in the economy and culture better explain the reemergence of for-profit imprisonment.

Money and Power: Tennessee's Privatization Subgovernment

In April 1997, Tennessee became the epicenter of the national prison privatization movement. That year, facing a projected $100 million budget shortfall, the Tennessee legislature gave serious consideration to privatizing the *entire* Tennessee state prison system—with an inmate population approaching twenty thousand (Hallett & Lee, 2000). On April 29, 1997, executives from Corrections Corporation of America escorted key members of the legislature's Select Oversight Committee (SOCC) on Corrections to a private meeting at the Crown Plaza Hotel, across from the state capitol in downtown Nashville. News reporters who accidentally learned of the meeting were politely asked to leave (Wade, 1997a). On April 30, 1997, executives from Wackenhut Corrections Corporation arrived in Nashville to take six members of the House Ways and Means Committee out to dinner.

So began the latest effort to "privatize" the Tennessee prison system. It had been tried before, when in 1985, after a federal court order forced the state to spend an additional $380 million on prison renovation and construction, Tom Beasley—former chairman of the Tennessee Republican Party—proposed to then Republican governor Lamar Alexander that his company, CCA, could "lock them up better, quicker, and for less" than the state (Kyle, 1998).

The major opponent to the latest effort to privatize Tennessee's prison system became the Tennessee State Employees' Association (TSEA). The TSEA is a state employee labor union, roughly forty-five hundred members of which serve as correctional officers in the state's prisons. Tennessee's experience with the effort to privatize its prisons affords a unique vantage point on both the national public policy debate about prison privatization as well as the very localized political connections established between private prison entrepreneurs and political leaders. As documented in Chapter 2, much the same types of relationships existed in the South during the establishment of the Convict Lease system (Curtin, 2000).

The events described here reveal a key truth about for-profit imprisonment: for-profit imprisonment is made possible through combinations of private and public interests that are less accountable and indeed less visible to citizens than their public prison counterparts. These networks involve combinations of private and governmental stakeholders that render imprisonment a *proprietary* rather than a *public* good.

Though many of the same forces driving the increase in for-profit imprisonment are also driving increases in public imprisonment, very real differences between the operational networks promoting each type of punishment and the programmatic goals of its constituents exist. Careful documentation of the interplay between state and nonstate actors in the development of punishments has long been a concern of sociologists of punishment, because it is this interplay that ultimately determines the character and social opinion of punishment itself (Goffman, 1961; Rusche & Kirchheimer, 1968; Welch, 2002, 2005; Garland, 2001a; Ericson et al., 1993; Shelden, 2001).

Insider Politics: The Context of Tennessee Prison Privatization

No system of power works by force alone, not even the law's last-resort power to punish. Instead it relies on meanings and symbols and representations that construe its own actions and weave them into the belief-systems, sensibilities, and cultural narratives of the social actors and audiences involved. Thus, to describe punishment as a form of power is not to tell the whole story.

—David Garland, "Punishment and Culture: The Symbolic Dimension of Criminal Justice"

The genesis of prison privatization in Tennessee must be understood in no uncertain terms as having been "mobilized" from within the local corporate and political power structure (Hallett & Lee, 2000). The key sponsors of the initiative were longtime political insiders, either current or former business partners, or otherwise connected through marriage or progeny. Tom Beasley and his cofounder of Corrections Corporation of America, Doctor R. Crants, were roommates at West Point. Beasley is a former chairman of the Tennessee Republican Party and occupied that position during the tenure of Republican governor Lamar Alexander. Alexander was governor in 1985, when CCA first proposed privatizing the entire Tennessee prison system. Early investors in CCA included Lamar Alexander's wife, Honey Alexander, and Lamar Alexander's successor as governor, Democrat Ned McWherter. At the time of CCA's founding, McWherter was the long-standing Speaker of the Tennessee House of Representatives.

In the most recent effort to privatize Tennessee's prisons, CCA worked directly with Representative Matt Kisber, who sponsored the bill, and who is part owner of a Nashville restaurant with subsequent Speaker of the House Jimmy Naifeh (Locker, 1997a). Naifeh's wife, Betty Anderson, as well as then Republican governor Don Sundquist's wife, Martha Sundquist, and the Sundquists' three adult children were business partners with Naifeh and Kisber in a Nashville restaurant. Governor Sundquist was on record as supporting prison privatization. Perhaps the most unseemly political connection in the affair, however, and certainly the connection that drew the most public attention, is the fact that the wife of the then Speaker of the House, Jimmy Naifeh, longtime supporter of prison privatization, and business partner of Beasley and Kisber was none other than Betty Anderson—CCA's chief lobbyist in the Tennessee legislature. All of this perhaps makes unsurprising the fact that Crants and Beasley were leading contributors to Governor Don Sundquist's reelection campaign in 1998—as well as contributors to Naifeh's and Kisber's reelection campaigns (Locker, 1997c).

Back in 1985, Governor Lamar Alexander was forced to call the legislature into a special session to deal with a federal court order placing a cap on the state's prison system. Like many states in the late 1970s, Tennessee began its own crusade to lower crime rates through the implementation of mandatory minimum sentencing. Predictably, this created the tremendous overcrowding that led to the federal court order placing limitations on how much prison space could be utilized without substantial improvement of conditions. By 1985 the situation had reached a crisis point, with rioting and several deaths and the declaration of the state's oldest prison in Nashville unconstitutional. Tennessee found itself very quickly in need of at least seven thousand additional prison beds and called for spending $380 million to build six new prisons (Tennessee Select Oversight Committee on Corrections, 1995).

It was during this period—during the special session—that Beasley introduced CCA's first proposal to manage the state's prison system. Beasley's 1985 statement to the legislature is worth repeating:

> Our proposal is simple—we will pay the state for the right to manage the system under the state's supervision; we will spend private capital to improve the system and draw our profit out of more efficient use of the state's regular operating budget. That is a $250 million—one quarter billion dollar turnaround in the state budget—without a tax increase! We believe this is absolutely a win-win situation and an unprecedented opportunity to make Tennessee a leader in this most difficult area. (Corrections Corporation of America, 1985, p. 2)

Sensing a potential battle for control over the correctional system with the governor, the state legislature saw fit to create the Tennessee Select Oversight Committee on Corrections, "a 10–member joint Senate and House committee charged with reviewing corrections plans, both capital and operational, to help ensure that the state delivers a correctional system that is effective and efficient." Fearing that too abrupt a move to privatize was short-sighted and legally risky, the legislature passed the Private Prison Contracting Act of 1986, which "limited the opportunity to privatize to a single, 180-bed state prison already under construction by the state" (Kyle, 1998).

Beasley's 1985 plan offered the state $100 million in cash for the right to manage the entire system with a ninety-nine-year lease, with the proviso that $250 million in capital expenditures be provided by CCA in exchange for a sum equal to the entire adult correctional budget for fiscal year 1986–1987—approximately $170 million (Kyle, 1998; Chesteen, 1998). Concerns about the constitutionality of prison privatization, and a Democrat-dominated legislature, helped forestall the push toward privatization. The Private Prison Contracting Act of 1986, however, left the door open for the privatization of future prisons (Kyle, 1998; Tennessee Select Oversight Committee on Corrections, 1995).

Finally, in 1991, Governor Ned McWherter authorized a contract for CCA to run the South Central Correctional Center in Clifton, Tennessee. The initial contract was for a three-year period, 1991–1994, mandating that "the performance of the contractor shall be compared to the performance of the State in operating similar facilities." The objective was to "compare public and private operation at basically the same type of physical plants." The legislation required a comparison of the performance and cost of the private operation to that of the state operation. Specifically, South Central would be compared to two other Tennessee facilities, Northwest Correctional Center and Northeast Correctional Center. "Importantly, for this comparative evaluation process, the three facilities being compared are nearly identical in physical space, design of housing units, infrastructure, support buildings, and administrative core" (Tennessee Select Oversight Committee on Corrections, 1995).

At the conclusion of the three-year contract, a report by the Tennessee Select Oversight Committee on Corrections—a report the U.S. General Accounting Office described as among the best comparative evaluations it had seen—became the subject of much controversy in the privatization debate (U.S. General Accounting Office, 1996). Although Tennesseans were never provided a thorough presentation of the estimated costs of the proposed operation of the entire prison system, several studies of individual Tennessee facilities existed by the time of the debate.[2]

The Three Public Deaths of the 1997 Initiative to Privatize Tennessee's Prison System

Strike One

Unfortunately, details like those offered above were not the central issues driving the privatization debate in Tennessee. Whereas the Tennessee media were quick to declare TSEA the victor, several crucial elements of the debate were never given adequate hearing. Certainly, the story of "secret meetings" that broke on April 29, 1997, marked the beginning of the debate—and gave those politicians involved much to answer for from a suspicious press. Several of the state's newspapers published editorials critical of the secret "closed-door" nature of those early meetings (Wade, 1997a, 1997b).

It was not the exclusion of the press or the TSEA, however, that proved to be the critical element in the first failure of the initiative—it was the exclusion of key members of the Democratic caucus in the Senate. At least three senators, including Steve Cohen, abruptly left when it became clear that the meeting was not open. When asked by a reporter (who had been excluded from the meeting) about the reason he was leaving, Cohen stated: "Enough has been done already that's not in the public eye. I don't think in the last three years we [Senate Democrats] have had a meeting on this issue. The bill has been done so much in secrecy at this point, everything ought to be open" (Sher, 1997).

By the time the bill's sponsors sought to rally the support of other legislators in early May 1997, only weeks remained until the end of the session. After the SOCC completed its review, the bill would have had to pass through both the House and the Senate Government and Finance Committees, and finally through the full legislature. Although the SOCC held two subsequent public hearings on the issue during this stage of the initiative, these hearings generated more heat than light—with a preacher from Memphis being escorted from the forum, loudly berating the relationship between the House Speaker and CCA's chief lobbyist. The lion's share of the hearings, however, were devoted to statements made by correctional officers organized by the TSEA. During these first hearings, TSEA firmly made the point that the SOCC's own study of South Central Correctional Center provided little evidence of either cost savings or enhanced performance. If savings could not be compellingly demonstrated for one facility—a primarily minimum-security facility at that—TSEA argued, how could the state rush to judgment on an effort to privatize the entire system (Hallett, 1997)?

Undeterred, Lieutenant Governor John Wilder introduced the bill in the Senate, attempting to unify Senate Democrats and appease criticism by the rank and file in the legislature. Said Wilder: "Some members of the Senate feel like they were left out. But nobody has been left out. The bill is now filed. This is the first official action. . . . Now its going to Corrections Oversight and that's where it's going to be reviewed. I want the Senate to know the Speaker is not pushing, the Speaker is presenting" (Locker, 1997b). After several meetings by the legislative sponsors attempting to revise various elements of the bill in time for a vote before the end of the session, too much time had passed, and Senator Jim Kyle announced that the bill could not be considered until July (Ferrar, 1997). Said Kyle: "The committee is going to come back in July and begin delving into this issue in an orderly fashion" (Locker, 1997b).

The first public death of the 1997 effort to privatize Tennessee's prison system had occurred. Mismanagement on the part of the bill's legislative sponsors, who relied on insider connections and a pro-privatization governor to carry the bill forward—rather than effectively lobbying the bill to the rank-and-file members of the House and Senate—proved to be the pivotal undoing of the initiative at this stage. As one senator put it (off the record to me): "That bill was dead on arrival—the most ineffectively lobbied bill I have ever seen. There was the sense in the rank and file that this came down from the top. . . . Now, we have big egos in the legislature and we don't like to be left out."

Strike Two

In July, the SOCC did indeed come back to the issue more systematically, holding additional hearings, during which private correctional service vendors presented their arguments in favor of privatization. The primary argument made by these vendors was that privatization would introduce "fair competition" into the operation of corrections and that such competition would enhance the performance of state-operated facilities as well as save the state money. It would be unwise, argued officials from Wackenhut Corrections Corporation, the other major vendor bidding on the contract aside from CCA, to offer one contract for the entire state to a single company. Multiple vendors and a gradual phasing in of privatization would offer the state more protection and a better bargaining position.

Estimates on the amount of money to be saved varied wildly, with initial claims by CCA of saving $100 million to revised claims of savings of up to $25 million. No specific numbers were ever presented publicly, however, because the proposals were again deemed "proprietary." The hired consultant to the SOCC ultimately suggested scaling back the initial proposal to privatize the entire system to privatizing 60 to 70 percent of the system.

Other proposed changes to the initial bill during this stage included a phasing in of privatization, with ultimately 30 percent to 40 percent of the state's prisons to be kept under state control. In other words, there would be no immediate carte blanche transfer of the entire prison system to a single private company. Moreover, there was wide agreement that private companies would be required to offer jobs to all current state prison system employees—though they could require work transfers to other facilities, a lessening of employee benefits, and the possibility that eventually some jobs would be eliminated.

By far the most important development during this stage of the initiative, however, was Governor Don Sundquist's proposal to restructure state oversight of corrections, with the creation of a new executive-branch state agency, the Tennessee Department of Criminal Justice. Under Sundquist's proposal, the governor would retain sole authority to authorize which prisons would be privatized or closed, as well as the terms under which privatized facilities would be managed, opened, and contracted for. Sundquist would also keep total control over the monitoring of contracts to private prison vendors, with monitoring officials from the new Department of Criminal Justice becoming part of the executive branch.[3]

In late October 1997, Democratic senator Jim Kyle, chair of the Tennessee Select Oversight Committee on Corrections, remarked about the possibility of the governor gaining complete control of the proposed privatization apparatus for the state: "As chairman of this committee, I'm uncomfortable with that idea" (Wade, 1997d). At that point the committee adjourned, scheduled to return to take a final vote on the legislation November 4–5, 1997. Meanwhile, the SOCC's consultant issued a report to the committee drawing into question vendors' claims that they could save the state up to 50 percent of its correctional operating budget. He also noted that the state's own Department of Corrections, if also allowed the flexibility of closing older facilities and building new ones, could cut its own costs by 30 percent.

On November 5, Senator Kyle announced: "The consensus on the committee is that there should be joint legislative and executive branch decision making on this venture. . . . Now we're waiting for the sponsors and the administration to come to an agreement" (Wade, 1997c). Here a key difference of opinion emerged between the bill's legislative sponsors and the SOCC, with cosponsor of the bill Representative Matt Kisber stating: "I feel that the executive branch, and the governor as the CEO of the executive branch, has to have the responsibility to run the departments vested in the administrative branch" (Wade, 1997d; see also Wade, 1997e). The legislature broke for holiday recess, with no action being taken on the bill. Later that day, Governor Sundquist issued a statement: "I'm not in favor of any dilution of my authority over prisons" (Wade, 1997e).

After the holidays and with the legislature back in session, Governor Sundquist indicated his intention to throw his full support behind yet a newer version of the bill drafted by his staff. This newest bill would be cosponsored by Representatives Matt Kisber and Page Walley, Lieutenant Governor John Wilder, and Senate Republican leader Ben Atchley. In Sundquist's new proposal, up to 70 percent of Tennessee's prisons could be privatized and would be monitored under the supervision of the proposed Tennessee Department of Criminal Justice—which would remain under the jurisdiction of the executive branch. In preparation for the debate, Sundquist appointed a five-member "advisory council" on prison privatization, including himself, Wilder, House Speaker Jimmy Naifeh, Finance Committee commissioner John Ferguson, and Comptroller William Snodgrass (P. West, 1998a).

With legislative leaders from the SOCC having invited a compromise from the governor and legislative sponsors before the holiday recess, legislative support for the effort was waning. In an effort to bolster the bill, Lieutenant Governor Wilder called another meeting—*to which all 132 Tennessee legislators were invited*—outlining the specifics of Sundquist's proposal. By early March 1998, SOCC members were hinting at their disapproval, with SOCC member Senator Bob Rochelle stating: "The [governor's] bill does not state any purpose, objective or goal the state is trying to accomplish by reorganizing the Department of Correction or expanding the state's authority to contract for prison management services" (Associated Press, 1998a).

On March 31, 1998, cosponsor Ben Atchley conceded that Sundquist's bill did not have the votes for passage in the Senate's State and Local

Government Committee. "We still have some work to do here," he stated. Atchley indicated, furthermore, that many legislators remained opposed to giving prison control to a new commissioner of criminal justice who worked for the governor under the auspices of a new Tennessee Department of Criminal Justice (P. West, 1998b).

Unable to garner the necessary committee votes, Sundquist's refusal to compromise effectively put the privatization initiative back to square one. Stated Atchley: "We lost the momentum. I think a fresh start may be what's needed" (Associated Press, 1998b). Atchley's cosponsor, Wilder, stated: "It's not ready to be passed. It's not over yet, but it's over for this session." A statement released on April 14 by the governor read: "The Governor still supports the concept of prison privatization and he plans to work legislatively and administratively to see that it happens" (Locker, 1998). About this time, the editorial cartoon below was published in the *Nashville Tennessean* (Figure 4.1).

Figure 4.1 Editorial cartoon depicting CCA's connection to the Tennessee state government. Used with permission. Copyright 1997 *Nashville Tennessean.*

Three Strikes and You're Out

With Lieutenant Governor John Wilder's promise to revive the privatization effort in the next legislative session quite clear, Tennesseans expected more wrangling over the issue in the fall of 1998. Governor Sundquist was the strong favorite for reelection in November, facing a little-known Democrat with one-tenth of the funding of the governor for his campaign. What Sundquist could not have predicted during this third phase of the initiative, however, was that CCA would provide the worst possible backdrop for political supporters of privatization: a seemingly unending series of news stories about escapes, murders, and riots in CCA facilities in Tennessee and around the country.

The first and most dramatic incident impacting local perception of CCA's competence was the set of events that took place at the Northeast Ohio Correctional Center in Youngstown. Several high-profile escapes and stabbings at that facility received intense media coverage in the Tennessee press. The local media immediately sought the reaction of legislative leaders to the events at CCA's Youngstown facility. Most damaging in the reports from Youngstown were allegations (subsequently proven) that the incidents involved inmates illegally transferred from Washington, D.C. Reports of high employee turnover and extreme violence at Youngstown saturated the news in Tennessee and raised additional questions about whether out-of-state inmates should be housed in Tennessee. There were roughly sixteen hundred out-of-state inmates in Tennessee's CCA facilities around the state at the time of the Youngstown incidents.

A number of reporters and one Democratic state senator, Pete Springer, ultimately traveled to Ohio to investigate the incidents. Springer ultimately returned to Ohio to offer testimony to the Ohio legislature on prison privatization problems in Tennessee (Hartmann, 1998). A key concern for Senator Springer was that the Youngstown incident seemed to revolve around a failure to select inmates for transfer according to their custody classification, that is, a failure to transfer the types of inmates specified in the contract. Springer made this a key plank in his reelection campaign, under way at the time. Representative Phil Pinion, a member of the SOCC, stated in the aftermath of these events: "The reaction I've gotten from members of the Tennessee legislature and the general public is it looks like we don't need to be going into something like privatization especially after what happened in Ohio" (Wade, 1998a).

In addition to the events in Ohio, however, several embarrassing and ill-timed incidents plagued CCA facilities in Tennessee. First, on September 4, 1998, a rapist managed to escape from Hardeman County Correctional Facility. Two weeks later, reports of a racially motivated stabbing incident at the same facility made headlines. Although the initial story released by CCA after the incident was that one inmate was hurt, a follow-up report indicated that the event was racially motivated and involved "about 70 inmates" (Aldrich, 1998).

Facing an election in roughly two months, key sponsors of the bill started to waver. Matt Kisber—sponsor of the original privatization legislation in 1997—stated in response to the reports from Youngstown:

> I think there is no question that the problems in Ohio make legislators more uncomfortable since they do not have information as to what is the cause of the problems and what could be done to prevent them. My advice to any private contractor doing business with a government entity is that disclosure is the best disinfectant. If there are problems, being under the light of sunshine tends to help find solutions to them. . . . If it's going to save money but risk public safety, that's not good enough. (ibid.)

Kisber's public withdrawal was a death blow: "Any time a primary proponent of an issue this controversial drops out, it does raise some concerns," said Representative Page Walley, a cosponsor of the revised bill (Wade, 1998a). Though first sticking firmly behind privatization—despite news of the events at Youngstown and in Tennessee, by the end of the month Governor Sundquist himself announced he would not pursue legislation authorizing prison privatization in the next legislative year, 1999. "There has been a lot of coverage and focus on recent incidents, on incident reporting and notification. There are some fair questions that have been raised that we think should be answered . . . and we didn't do a good job of quantifying cost savings" (Wade, 1998b).

In sum, mismanagement on the part of the privatization initiative's legislative sponsors—and on the part of CCA itself—had more to do with the demise of the proposal to privatize Tennessee's prison system than did any grassroots-level opposition to privatization organized by the state employees' union or other activists (see Hallett & Lee, 2000). The Tennessee State Employee's Association was vocal with legislators and visible with protests, but this public activism had little to do with the actual failure of the privatization effort. Betty Anderson, chief lobbyist for CCA, stated after the bill's withdrawal: "I have to congratulate the state employees group. They did a good job amassing their numbers" (Locker, 1998). Her statement belies CCA's own role in driving the final stake through the heart of the initiative. Though the effort to privatize Tennessee's prisons did not provide for a thorough debate on the substantive issues of prison privatization for Tennessee citizens, it did raise serious concerns about the ability of private prisons to be held publicly accountable.

Norman Rockwell to the Rescue: The Capitalist Ecology of CCA Redux

> The power exerted by a legal regime consists less in the force that it can bring to bear against violators of its rules than in its capacity to persuade people that the world described in its images and categories is the only attainable world in which a sane person would want to live.
>
> —Robert Gordon, *Critical Legal Histories*

Stinging from the legislative sponsors' withdrawal of support for the effort to hand over control of Tennessee's prison system to CCA, the company ran a series of eleven full-page ads in the (Gannett-owned) *Nashville Tennessean,* the state's largest circulating newspaper and "paper of record," from October 25 through November 19, 1998, and a series of television commercials on Nashville stations throughout the same period. As shown in Chapter 3, the newspaper ads themselves were explicitly Rockwellian, evocative of Norman Rockwell's mercantile suburban American dream.

In the aftermath of the escapes and riots plaguing CCA facilities across the country, in each of the ads aimed at Tennesseans, CCA sought to reassure the public of its commitment to public safety over profit—as well as to counter the charges of racist and capitalistic exploitation of nonviolent minority offenders leveled at the company by activists. Seven of the ads feature either African Americans or Hispanics.

Forsaken People and Places: Privatization and Dispossession

The argument presented here draws heavily on the research of those documenting that the drug war, as the fountainhead of most private prison revenue in America, cannot be understood outside of the context of race. Are we headed again into an era where we become a "land of prisoners and keepers," as Scott Christianson refers to Puritan-era America and its practices of slavery and indenture in his recent book *With Liberty for Some: 500 Years of Imprisonment in America?* Are we solving the problems we need to solve or exacerbating fundamental problems by ignoring them for profit? As criminologists Ed McGarrell and Thomas Castellano muse:

> The demand for punishment of individual offenders fails to address the structural sources of crime. Crime thus continues relatively unaffected by policy and the demand for punishment escalates. Similarly, as the demand for punishment is translated into crime control policy, the criminal justice system, for organizational and justice reasons, is constrained from full implementation and the legitimation deficit escalates leading to further pressure for punishment. (McGarrell & Castellano, 1991, p. 191)

As shown by the recent case of Tennessee, public hatred of criminals provides perhaps the best-possible basis for converting public money into private hands—but at what cost? Beyond proposals prescribed by the relatively few people capable of making a short-term profit from incarceration, governmental facilitation of prison privatization arguably amounts to malfeasance of duty (by the government's failure to devise means by which crime is reduced, rather than accommodated and profited on through privatization).

At its current stage of development, the debate about prison privatization is unfortunately preoccupied with short-term "micromanagement" issues such as per diem costs, contract monitoring, cost savings through employee benefit reductions, and so on—and hardly attentive to the longer-term "macropolicy" issues raised by its emergence. These micropolicy issues are the subject of Chapter 6. Essentially, we are missing the forest for the trees, in that we have given over deliberation on ways to reduce crime in favor of making profit on ever larger numbers of offenders.

In the area of correctional policy making in particular, it is well documented that localized power and influence play a disproportionately instrumental role in determining policy outcomes, primarily because there tend to be fewer at-large stakeholders involved in the development of correctional policy than in other areas of governmental action (Gilbert, 2000a; DiIulio, 1993; Stoltz, 1997; Palumbo, 1986, 1994; Wittenberg, 1996). As a leading critic of prison privatization, John DiIulio, puts it, specifically relating to the privatization issue:

Most of the time, it is the corrections commissioner and a handful of executive and legislative branch officials who set the correctional policy agenda, make decisions, and oversee their implementation. In certain jurisdictions, the officials who make corrections policy are influenced by certain outside (nongovernmental) persons and groups. They form what political scientists call "subgovernments": clusters of individuals that effectively make most of the routine decisions in a given area of policy. (1993, p. 137; see also Stoltz, 1997, for an elaboration of "subgovernmental" influence on correctional policy making in the context of prison privatization)

In sum, the particular case of prison privatization in Tennessee documents the self-serving and agentistic behavior of political and corporate elites exerting disproportionate influence in the correctional policy formation process—while also coproducing arguments about the causes of crime and about the legitimacy of the capitalistic social order. The cooperation of legislative and corporate elites in the drafting of the legislation intended to transfer the public prison system into private hands and overtures by Corrections Corporation of America raise troubling questions about the simple "crime control" utility of prisons and of for-profit prisons in particular. Pondered in this way, the Tennessee case study reveals the truth of Emile Durkheim's argument that certain segments of society both rely on and benefit from crime—and that criminality itself, in surprising ways, is an exploitable social resource for many in our society, including criminologists (see Chapter 2; Durkheim, 1933; Beckett, 1997; and Chambliss, 2001).

Punishment, Capitalism, and Race: "Controlling the Dangerous Classes"

The fact that our "crime wars" center almost exclusively on the behaviors of inner-city minorities sends a socially revealing signal about our "crime consciousness."[1] As Garland states: "Penality communicates meaning not just about crime and punishment but also about power, authority, legitimacy, normality, morality, personhood, social relations and a host of other tangential matters" (1991, 195). Putting large numbers of black men once again into for-profit prisons reveals something about *today's* prevailing social order. Private prisons reveal truths about our culture and social system that have little to do with crime control, but have much to do, instead, with the often racist and exploitative character of our capitalistic economic system. American culture powerfully works to structure existing social arrangements between classes of people (that is, whites and blacks, rich and poor, men and women), making power imbalances seem normal, if not acceptable (Surette, 1998).

The mass incarceration of African American men is now so ubiquitous and prevalent that it has become an accepted social fact; crime is now cast largely as a "black" problem (Davis, 1998). CCA's advertisements, of course, both play upon and amplify this public perception. As such, real solutions to crime control that seek not merely to warehouse offenders but also to improve social conditions and well-being by addressing the underlying causes of crime are unlikely to gain support.

Many critics of the modern criminal justice system argue that its workings are devoted less to reducing crime than to providing politicians and other entrepreneurs a symbolic means of justifying their own existence. By identifying "suitable enemies" deserving of social action, entrepreneurs of this sort develop and implement reactive policies inadequate to the task of effecting real social change, thereby perpetuating the "need" for prisons and fueling public outrage (Wacquant, 1999; see also Beckett, 1997; Chambliss, 2001; Sherman, 1983; Christie, 1993; and Gusfield, 1963).

In sum, despite decades of research demonstrating that increased spending on expanded imprisonment and longer prison terms have little impact on crime, public spending on just these activities has dominated criminal justice policy over the past thirty years (RAND, 1997; Rose & Clear, 1998). Add to this the reorganization of the former Immigration and Naturalization Service and its placement under the umbrella of the new Department of Homeland Security, and we realize that the "prison industrial complex" may well one day come to rival the military industrial complex—or, worse yet, become indistinguishable from it (Welch, 2005). Add to that our already well-documented cultural history of keeping marginalized and purportedly threatening "others" subject to the highest levels of social control—and renewed for-profit imprisonment in the twenty-first century becomes more easily explained. Put another way, our problem is more serious than even that of having a secretive cabal of powerful and unaccountable military leaders goad us into unnecessary defense spending: the oppressive policies of which we speak take place from the ground up, as it were, with the full participation of local communities and local legal authorities with no direct ties to for-profit prison entrepreneurs. Our problem, in a word, is cultural.

FIVE

Bad Faith: A Critical Look at "Faith-Based" Corrections

When historians talk of the cultural forces which have influenced penal policy, the forces which they have in mind are most often religion and humanitarianism.

—David Garland, *Punishment and Modern Society: A Study in Social Theory*

Proponents of "faith-based" correctional programming argue that, as President George W. Bush recently stated, "once a life is broken, it can only be rebuilt by another caring, concerned human being." As shown below, however, proponents of faith-based correctional programming actually seek to reduce government spending on amelioration social programs in the context of "welfare reform"—placing faith-based programming inside a political platform hostile to the tradition of providing government resources to the poorest among us. In other words, faith-based programs are very much a part of an ideological agenda supportive of the transfer of public wealth into private hands. This chapter argues that faith-based corrections is another in a long line of criminal justice appropriations of religious symbolism that divide people into the "Godly" and "Godless," "moral" and "immoral"—for political and "other" purposes understood as separate from "crime control." Indeed, as this chapter will show, faith-based corrections seek to simultaneously diminish social responsibility for the poor while fostering further elements of privatization in the correctional enterprise. Regardless of the merits of faith in helping someone overcome criminality, faith-based corrections programs are an important piece of the contemporary correctional privatization puzzle.

Because the research perspective in this book is premised on the notion that prisons serve many social functions *other* than crime control, other social purposes of faith-based correctional programming must be explored. This chapter identifies faith-based correctional initiatives as the latest conservative definition of the crime problem and as a "symbolic crusade" orchestrated by "moral entrepreneurs" (Gusfield, 1963; Becker, 1963). Drawing on literature exploring status politics and symbolic crusades, this chapter examines the general claims made by proponents of faith-based corrections and the specific elements of faith-based legislation recently passed in Florida. The chapter concludes with an analysis of these claims as compared to the academic evidence on the causes and ecological distribution of crime.

Moral Entrepreneurs and Symbolic Crusades: A Framework for Analysis

> It is appropriate to think of reformers as crusaders because they typically believe their mission is a holy one. The prohibitionist serves as an excellent example, as does the person who wants to suppress vice and sexual delinquency or the person who wants to do away with gambling. Many moral crusades have strong humanitarian overtones. The crusader is not only interested in seeing to it that other people do what he thinks is right. He believes that if they do what he thinks is right it will be good for them.
>
> —Howard Becker, *Outsiders: Studies in the Sociology of Deviance*

First published in 1963, Joseph Gusfield's book on Prohibition titled *Symbolic Crusade: Status Politics and the American Temperance Movement* became an instant classic. The book compellingly suggests that criminalization of the production and consumption of alcohol in the United States during Prohibition was skillfully orchestrated by rural middle-class Protestants seeking to reassert their particular values over and above the increasing influence of urban, lower-class Catholics in

American culture. According to Gusfield, the actual goal of Prohibition was to elevate the status of the group promoting it (rural, middle-class Protestants), rather than to control the abuse of alcohol by those they suggested used too much of it (namely, urban, lower-class Catholics) (Vold et al., 1998, p. 229).

"Symbolic crusades" should be seen, according to Gusfield, as a kind of social drama emphasizing the role of "status as a political interest" over and above any instrumental or material gain a crusading group might seek (1963, p. 167). Such crusades embody attempts by "moral entrepreneurs," working on behalf of discernable groups, to elevate their own status—by characterizing the social behaviors of "others" as somehow threatening to or deviant from the dominant culture. Howard Becker defines "moral entrepreneurs" as people seeking to preserve or elevate their own status by making it their business to identify "evils" in society "about which something ought to be done" (1963, p. 153; see also Welch, 1999).

A consistent criticism of *Symbolic Crusade*, however, has been that it overemphasized the importance of status as a distinct political objective and that it underemphasized the instrumental nature of crusaders' activities in the public sphere (see especially Rumsbarger, 1989). As Kurt Lang wrote in his 1964 review of *Symbolic Crusade:* "The changing fortunes of this movement and its ideology are here interpreted in terms of status politics, a concept that came into vogue more rapidly than it could be defined." Whereas class politics, according to Gusfield, are "instrumentally oriented toward the allocation of material resources," symbolic crusades are based on status politics, where "it is not economic gain but the prestige of a life style that is at stake" (p. 768). As Mayer Zald also states: "Gusfield ignores the fact that many economic or class-based conflicts transform themselves into status politics. When ideologies develop to justify differential claims on the distribution of rewards, prestige and the normative order are not long ignored. While there are differences between status politics and class politics, the differences are not as sharp as Gusfield maintains" (1964, p. 392).[1]

In sum, as subsequent critiques of Gusfield's work have revealed, moral crusades are seldom driven solely by their purported symbolic objectives; rather, they are also at heart a form of power politics with both symbolic and instrumental aims (see Rouse & Unnithan, 1993; and especially Rumsbarger, 1989). More recent applications in the literature on status politics have focused directly on the instrumental objectives of symbolic crusades. In the most elaborate work, historian John

Rumsbarger explores the instrumentalist agenda of capitalist elites in the promotion and support of Prohibition, characterizing the legal implementation of Prohibition as being driven primarily by industrialist concerns over worker turnover and productivity. Indeed, Rumsbarger goes so far as to state as his mission "to challenge as directly as possible the notion that temperance reform was merely a status concern of the middle classes," concluding: "Without capital's need for profit there would have been no liquor question or temperance movement as they came to be in America" (1989, pp. xix, 188).

As George B. Vold, Thomas J. Bernard, and Jeffrey Snipes point out, "Since campaigns against deviance usually result in the redistribution of benefits from some groups (the deviants) to others (the promoters and supporters of the campaigns), it seems likely that the social solidarity produced depends at least partially on the solidification of power relationships in the society" (1998, p. 230). This chapter utilizes the research mentioned above to interpret the emergence of faith-based corrections as a symbolic crusade with both resource- and status-focused objectives. Here, Gusfield is worth quoting at length:

> The struggle to control the symbolic actions of government is often as bitter and as fateful as the struggle to control its tangible effects. Much of our response to political events is in terms of their dramatic, symbolic meaning. This is especially the case where elements of the status order are at issue. The distribution of prestige is partially regulated by symbolic acts of public and political figures. Such persons "act out" the drama in which one status group is degraded and another is given deference. In seeking to effect their honor and prestige in the society, a group makes demands upon governing agents to act in ways which serve to symbolize deference or to degrade the opposition whose status they challenge or who challenge theirs. (1963, p. 167)

The Context of Faith-Based Initiatives: Scaling Back the Welfare State

Drugs are destroying more children and more families than poverty ever did.

—President George W. Bush, 2001, at the nomination of John Walters to direct the Office of Drug Control Policy

Attendant with the agenda of faith-based corrections is a lessening of governmental responsibility for social welfare and an attribution of *immo-*

rality as the ultimate cause of crime and poverty (Wilson, 1996, 1999). As such, faith-based programming is associated with broader calls by conservatives to lower taxes, eliminate government jobs through privatization, and promote "individual responsibility" as the best remedy for social problems.

As mentioned in Chapter 4, Barry Goldwater is often credited with successfully recasting the "crime problem" from one involving economic marginality and lack of opportunity to one caused by a society in the throes of individual moral decay (Parenti, 1999; Beckett, 1997; Epstein, 1977). In the course of this transformation in the definition of the crime problem also came a redefinition of the solution: harsher sentences and more police, more punishment and less "rehabilitation." In the process of orchestrating what later came to be known as the "war on crime," conservative activists successfully recharacterized crime control from being a primarily *local and preventative* enterprise to one necessitating federal government involvement as a matter of "national security," as President George H. W. Bush once put it. As a result of these definitional changes, a shift in responsibility for solving the crime problem occurred as well. Crime was no longer viewed as a "social problem" best understood and dealt with by "experts," but as an issue of national well-being and security appropriately handled by politicians. As stated earlier, crime became a moral issue much more so than one of policy design, economy, or law (Clear, 1997). In this context, punishment soon became the dominant and most frequently prescribed solution, even by otherwise "liberal" politicians.

As Gusfield concludes near the end of *Symbolic Crusade:* "When issues are structured in moral terms they become tests of status. In the context of cultural conflicts, the moralization of issues places the prestige of each status-bearing group at stake" (1963, p. 147). Thus, the extent to which public debate about crime is successfully reduced to moralistic tenets focused on individual responsibility is the extent to which macro-level definitions of its causes are able to be cast off as "soft" or pathetically weak. The symbolic power of the crime issue proved too much for politicians of both major political parties to ignore. As mentioned above, incarceration rates rose faster under Democratic president Bill Clinton than under either Republican George H. W. Bush or his Republican predecessor, Ronald Reagan.

Once More with Feeling: Shifting Blame and Playing the Race Card

> I visit churches and charities serving their neighbors nearly everywhere I go in this country. And nothing is more exciting or encouraging. Every day they prove that our worst problems are not hopeless or endless. Every day they perform miracles of renewal. Wherever we can, we must expand their role and reach, without changing them or corrupting them. It is the next, bold step of welfare reform. . . . We must apply our conservative and free-market ideas to the job of helping real human beings.
>
> —President George W. Bush, quoted in *Compassionate Conservatism: What It Is, What It Does, and How It Can Transform America*, by Marvin Olasky

Inasmuch as crime has been a good issue for politicians, it has also funneled tremendous resources into state coffers for prison construction, the hiring of more police officers, and longer prison sentences (Beckett, 1997; Petersilia, 1994). The vast majority of resources spent in the war on crime, of course, have gone to public and governmental agencies. Numerous elements of faith-based programming, however, seek to redirect government spending away from public agencies and funnel them to private organizations outside of government. By suggesting that activities engaged in by faith-based groups (for example, drug rehabilitation and job-placement programs) produce better results than similar programs run by the government, proponents of faith-based programming rely on claims of superior performance and morality. The preamble to Florida's 2001 Criminal Rehabilitation Bill—in which the term *faith-based* appears fifty-five times in its twenty-three-page text—demonstrates the characteristic agenda of conservatives over the past twenty-five years: to attribute social problems to personal failings and to take *government* out of the business of fixing them.

> Whereas state government should not and cannot bear the sole burden of treating and helping those suffering from addictions and self-injurious behaviors, and, Whereas, faith-based organizations are "armies of compassion" devoted to changing individuals' hearts and lives and can offer cost-effective substance abuse treatment through the use of volunteers and other cost saving measures, and Whereas research has proven that "one-on-one" private and faith-based programming is often more effective than government programs in shaping and reclaiming lives because they are free to assert the essential connection between responsibility

and human dignity; their approach is personal, not bureaucratic; their service is not primarily a function of professional background, but of individual commitment; and they inject an element of moral challenge and spiritual renewal that government cannot duplicate and Whereas, in an effort to transform lives and break the personally destructive and expensive recidivism cycle, Florida should increase the number of chaplains who strengthen volunteer participation and expand the pilot [faith-based] dormitory program that includes a voluntary faith component that supports inmates as they reenter communities. . . . Be It Enacted by the Legislature of the State of Florida. (2001 Fl. ALS 110; 2001 Fla. Laws ch. 110; 2001 Fla. SB 912)

In this example of faith-based legislation, the state is removed from its traditional responsibility over crime control, with private "cost-effective" "armies of compassion" that will "change hearts" sharing the burden. The "moral challenge" put forward by prison chaplains and their volunteers, moreover, treats the problems of crime and addiction as simply moral failings unrelated to issues of economic inequality or social structure—ignoring decades of research documenting that both criminality and addiction are concentrated in the most socioeconomically disadvantaged neighborhoods (Currie, 1993; Sampson & Raudenbush, 2001). In short, faith-based programming of this type treats crime and addiction in a very narrowly construed "religious" way. Faith-based programming operates as a religiously sanctioned means of lessening collective (state) responsibility for solving social problems through mechanisms of cost savings (that is, tax reduction) and diversion of resources to groups outside of the government. The sitting governor of Florida at the time the faith-based legislation passed was the president's brother, Jeb Bush.

Instrumental Objectives of Faith-Based Groups

Invocation of the benevolent symbols of religion, of course, is nothing new for criminal justice. Indeed, justice programming has been steeped in religious imagery from the time of the Quakers and before (see Morris & Rothman, 1995). Religious themes have frequently been mobilized by moral entrepreneurs to describe behaviors as "immoral," particularly those behaviors associated with marginalized or threatening members of the population, such as children in need of "saving" or alcohol users in need of abstinence (Platt, 1977; Gusfield, 1963).

Howard Becker writes: "The most obvious consequence of a successful crusade is the creation of a new set of rules. With the creation of a new set of rules we often find that a new set of enforcement agencies and officials is established. With the establishment of organizations of rule enforcers, the crusade becomes institutionalized" (1993, 24). As Marvin Olasky recently suggested, the heart of the faith-based agenda embodies a set of very instrumental goals for faith-based groups: "regulatory reform, tax code incentives for charitable contributions, and non-discrimination in grant making" (quoted in Carr, 2001).

In addition to creating the Office of Faith-Based and Community Initiatives as a means of institutionalizing access for religious groups to government funding, the Bush administration released a fascinating report suggesting that faith-based organizations have suffered from "systematic discrimination" and recommending that the government "level the playing field" (Cooper, 2001; White House Printing Office, 2001, p. 5). In language highly (and highly ironically) reminiscent of the civil rights movement, the White House report admonishes Congress to act on the pending legislation as a matter of fundamental fairness. As a *Los Angeles Times* story reporting President Bush's initial announcement of John DiIulio as the director of the Office of Faith-Based and Community Initiatives reveals, the proponents of faith-based programming have successfully mobilized their cause: "When President Bush unveiled his long-promised plan to give federal money to faith-based organizations that help the poor and troubled, he was keeping one of his earliest campaign pledges to religious conservatives" (Cooper, 2001, p. 15).

As Bush campaign adviser and University of Texas journalism professor Marvin Olasky explains in his book *Compassionate Conservatism*, supporters of faith-based programming had a specific instrumental objective: to give religious service providers access to federal funds reserved primarily for non-faith-based organizations. Olasky claims that a "curious interpretation of the 1st Amendment" dominated Washington programs in the 1960s. Funding programs that "marginalized God" and "demanded that workers check their religion at the door" also "froze out" faith-based programs. He concludes: "Even licensing, the government's seal of approval, could readily be withheld from an organization whose counselors believed strongly enough in their faith to share it with strangers. Government funds could be used by religious groups, but only if they set up religion-less government look-alikes that were rarely effective. With many first-rate programs out of bounds, government often bought into the second rate" (2000, p. 176).

As Olasky reports in his book, which includes both a foreword and an afterword using campaign material from Bush for President, Inc., a coalition of religious leaders, politicians, and social scientists coalesced around this notion of faith-based programming and actively developed its agenda (2000, p. 13). Early supporters of "compassionate conservatism" were fiscal conservatives such as former representative Newt Gingrich and Senator John Ashcroft (see ibid.), noted for their willingness to shut down the federal government rather than raise taxes (Woodward, 1996). By 1998, a prominent group of conservatives met privately with candidate Bush to develop the themes of the faith-based agenda, including Reagan-era criminologist James Q. Wilson, Bush Sr.–era drug czar William Bennett, and future director of the Office of Faith-Based and Community Initiatives, John J. DiIulio (Olasky, 2000, p. 13). Olasky's earlier tome, *The Tragedy of American Compassion*, was used as the "proof" that welfare benefits needed to be time limited for those "able" to work—regardless of whether they can actually find work (Wilson, 1999; Reich, 2002). In the booming economy of the 1990s, more (low-paying) jobs were available for even marginal workers.

It is worth pointing out at this juncture that President George W. Bush's director of the Office of Drug Control Policy, John Walters, was chief of staff to the first president Bush's drug czar, William Bennett. Moreover, Bennett coauthored a book with DiIulio and Walters titled *Body Count: Moral Poverty and How to Win America's War against Crime and Drugs* (1996), in which the authors label certain juvenile offenders "superpredators," deserving of adult-level punishments. DiIulio was also a prominent advocate of mandatory minimum sentences (Cooper, 2001).[2] Walters later served as President George W. Bush's director of Drug Control Policy (the "drug czar").

Central to the policy of shifting taxpayer resources away from the government and into the private sector, of course, is the claim that faith-based groups actually do provide better services in the realm of crime prevention and rehabilitation. At this early point in the development of faith-based programming, it would be useful to cross-examine the academic evidence surrounding the two fundamental claims of its proponents: that poverty and crime are best explained by individual lack of morality and that private groups deliver better services to offenders than do those from the public sector.

Although it is not the central focus of this chapter, a related question is whether "religiosity" itself may be causally linked to lower crime rates.

The subject of intense academic debate, researchers are seeking to "test whether the effects of religiosity on delinquency [and adult criminality] are spurious or completely indirect via social bonding, social learning, and socio-demographic variables" (Johnson, Larson, De Li, & Jang, 2000b). That is, if religiosity is associated with church attendance, are the social networks and resources generated by church membership the *real* cause of lowered criminality (what social-disorganization theorists like John Hagan [1994] call human and social capital), or is the religious conversion itself the cause? Moreover, are offenders who "find religion" somehow qualitatively different from those who do not, making studies of "convict converts" subject to selection bias? Studies can be found suggesting both that religiosity does reduce some criminality (Evans, Cullen, & Dunaway, 1995; Johnson et al., 2000a) and that it does not (Johnson et al., 2000b).

Crime and Social Disorganization

Perhaps the most heavily researched theme in all of criminology is the "class-crime connection"—the notion that conditions associated with economic deprivation and poverty causally elevate levels of criminality (Seigel, 2001, p. 68). A key argument of social-disorganization theory is that when localities become "unable to provide essential services, such as education, health care, and proper housing . . . they experience significant levels of unemployment, single parent-families, and families on welfare" (p. 191). One way of coping with these deficiencies, social-disorganization theorists argue, is through the utilization of illegal avenues of economic production, such as the drug trade (Byrne & Sampson, 1986). Arguably, by not giving "at-risk" communities the resources they need to overcome the limitations that condition their lives, we perpetuate the problem of crime. Socially disorganized communities often have high rates of criminality due to the fact that the social and human capital available to residents that might help them succeed through legal avenues is limited. Moreover, as public resources are diverted toward prisons and away from public programs in education and child care, for example, socially disadvantaged communities struggle all the more.

Conclusion: Privatization, Devolution, and
Faith-Based Corrections

Inasmuch as "immoral" behavior has been made the focal point of the U.S. crime problem, strategies for addressing it through social programs and economic development become less politically viable. As noted above, in the United States, symbolic crusades have relied upon moralistic attributions of behavior while advancing a resource-focused policy agenda affirming the worldview of its adherents. Indeed, associating social problems with personal *immorality* has become a signature framework for scaling back social programs by both major political parties—successfully neutralizing decades of research linking crime and other social problems *first* to social disorganization and poverty (Wilson, 1999, 1996; Currie, 1993).

The "immoral character–drug use" formulation for understanding crime and poverty, of course, is nothing new. Nancy Reagan's "Just Say No" campaign has also been characterized as a symbolic crusade, one that "focused on controlling alcohol and drug use, but also included moral judgements as to the causes of such behavior" (Rouse & Unnithan, 1993, p. 219). Significant amounts of social research, however, point to the inverse causal model: that of *poverty* as the primary cause of drug abuse, and poverty as the most important variable structuring the pervasiveness of crime in the poorest communities. As Elliot Currie concludes: "The link between drug abuse and deprivation is one of the strongest in forty years of careful research. I am not suggesting that drug abuse is confined to the poor. But the evidence consistently tells us that endemic drug use is not randomly or evenly distributed in the United States or elsewhere. The American drug problem is often portrayed as if it were classless. This classless imagery distorts the reality of hard-drug abuse and hobbles our ability to come to grips with it" (1993, p. 77).

The agenda devolving state responsibility for social welfare to entities outside the government also involves the strategic assignment of *public* resources to well-connected *private* groups. This faith-based privatization, in particular, not only shifts responsibility for social welfare away from the state but also casts social welfare itself as the individualized product of *moral* versus *immoral* agents. Services once offered exclusively by the state to address "social" problems are now devolved to private groups addressing what are cast as individual moral failings. Marginalized social groups, therefore, are unable to have their status viewed as the product of social forces *larger* than individual human beings, but instead bear the mark of an immoral, *even ungodly,* condition. Social welfare essentially becomes a "private" issue between oneself and one's God and the nongovernmental organizations trying to help. The hallmark governmental function of ensuring the public good is, thereby, forfeited to private groups having access to both public resources *and* God.

The latest conservative definition of the crime problem may be understood to be faith based—marking religiously affiliated programs worthy of funding, while characterizing those that are merely "governmental" as ineffective bureaucracy and lower in the "status order." Concordant with this attribution degrading governmentally sponsored programming for communities and offenders, in favor of programs offered by faith-based groups themselves, *have been significant changes to the rules* governing allocation of resources and the institutionalized prominence of faith-based programs themselves. Although concerns over separation of church and state—and the possibility that accepting money from government actually *compromises* the faith-based agenda of churches—have come up, they are not the focus of this chapter. This chapter, instead, has concerned itself with the attributions of faith-based legislation seeking to scale back governmental spending on offender rehabilitation and treatment, while funneling resources to private faith-based groups—all on the presumption that criminality is ultimately caused by a lack of morals. As such, the faith-based initiative described here contains both status- and resource-focused elements similar to symbolic crusades of the past.

Ironically, whereas politicians of both parties have embraced "getting tough on crime" and have rejected rehabilitation and endorsed privatization, a central element of "faith-based programming" in prisons is designed to be *rehabilitative.* Indeed, Corrections Corporation of America itself has widely implemented faith-based programming and calls it rehabilitative! Says one of CCA's faith-based promoters, David Bradby, a CCA vice president: "We hope to create a culture where inmates can reflect on their spiritual lives. Inmates will experience up to 732 hours of faith-based activities after six months in the program. Activities include journaling, character work, anger management courses, community service, mentoring, and optional worship services and study groups." As quoted in a promotional piece for CCA: "Bradby says the program's intent is to enhance inmate rehabilitation and quality of life, and ease inmate transition into society, with the ultimate aim of decreasing costs associated with recidivism, crime and overcrowding" (Corrections Corporation of America, 2003).

Why is it that some (faithful?) offenders are suddenly worthy of rehabilitation and others (the Godless) are not? Is rehabilitation rather than strict warehousing and punishment of inmates coming back into vogue? The comment above illustrates again the repeated pattern of interested stakeholders appropriating the modes of punishment for their own purposes.

SIX

The Easy Inmate Market: The Micropolitics of Private Prisons

But no one's hand can wipe away those tears
he sheds invisibly today, which one hears in his
laughter and in his speech and in his songs. I know
what the world has done to my brother and how
narrowly he has survived it. And I know, which
is much worse, and this is the crime of which I
accuse my country and my countrymen, and for
which neither I nor time nor history will ever forgive
them, that they have destroyed and are destroying
hundreds of thousands of lives and do not know it.

—James Baldwin, "My Dungeon Shook," in *The
Fire Next Time*

Forces Driving Contemporary Prison Privatization

As a result of the late-twentieth-century's dramatic increase in incarceration documented in Chapter 1, correctional administrations at all three levels of government (federal, state, and local) turned to private for-profit corporations to manage their burgeoning number of inmates in privately operated correctional facilities. In addition to the introduction of private contractors into the operation of prisons, however, during this period many units of government from local to federal increasingly sought to privatize other formerly public service functions, including waste disposal, education, mass transit, infrastructure repair, and construction (Gilbert, 2000a; Touche Ross & Co., 1987). As discussed below, however, the privatization of *prisons* is a unique phenomenon, imposing unique burdens and responsibilities upon its constituent parties. In the realm of private operation and management of prisons, privatization has taken place in three key areas (see Shichor, 1995):

1. Private financing and construction of prisons, particularly to avoid the need for issuing public bonds to finance construction of new facilities.
2. Private industry involvement inside prisons, particularly in the provision of services to prisoners and in the utilization of prisoners as laborers.
3. Private management, construction, and operation of whole prison facilities by independent contractors.

This chapter addresses contemporary policy issues related to the latter form of privatization—that of privately held firms managing, operating, and sometimes owning entire correctional facilities on a for-profit basis.

Mandatory Sentencing and Mass Imprisonment

The "war on crime" undertaken by both conservative and liberal administrations, beginning with Lyndon Johnson in the mid-1960s and lasting all through the 1990s, brought with it a profound shift in incarceration policy. In this relatively short period of time, penal responses to offending shifted entirely—from being focused on indeterminate "rehabilitative" practices to determinate and lengthy mandatory minimum sentences (Quinney, 1974, pp. 60–81). "Determinate" or "mandatory minimum" sentencing resulted in both a lengthening in the average duration of time served by offenders, as well as a reduction in the level of discretion provided judges and parole boards (Clear & Cole, 1994, p. 81).

As incarceration rates increased, prisons became more overcrowded and costly. In the 1960s, politicians also began to recognize the salience of crime for voters, concentrating major portions of their political agenda on crime control (Parenti, 1999). Over time, in part because of cost, prisons became almost exclusively custodial—"warehouses" for large numbers of prisoners. As Jerome Miller documents, by 1993, African Americans dominated the prison population, constituting 55 percent of inmates nationwide. Miller and others attribute this renewed hyperincarceration of African Americans to the drug war itself (Miller, 1996, p. 55; Tonry, 1995; Rose & Clear, 1998).

It is important to note as well that the expanded use of incarceration during this period was *not the result of increasing crime rates,* but rather the result of shifts in criminal justice policy (Bohm & Haley, 1997, p. 327; Austin & Irwin, 2001; Petersilia, 1994; Donziger, 1996). In other words, the skyrocketing incarceration rate was brought about *not by an explosion in the level of crime,* but rather a *shift in philosophy* regarding how best to respond to crime. We rather suddenly began to punish a broader spectrum of crimes more severely. As drug-related crimes became the particular target of mandatory minimum sentencing schemes in the 1980s—with even nonviolent drug crimes such as possession of marijuana being assigned mandatory minimum prison sentences in numerous states—the proportion of African Americans incarcerated increased dramatically (Donziger, 1996, pp. 15, 25).

In a study of incarceration rates in California, for example, the state with the nation's highest rate of incarceration, Joan Petersilia concludes that public fear of crime, rather than actual increases in the rate of crime, best explain the adoption of mandatory sentencing schemes in that state. According to Petersilia, as fear of crime increased,

> the nation shifted its focus away from addressing the "root causes" of crime and the rehabilitation of criminals toward making crime penalties more severe. . . . The state passed the Determinate Sentencing Law in 1977, which, among other things, embraced punishment as the purpose of prison, required mandatory prison sentences for many offenses formerly eligible for probation, and dramatically increased the rate at which probation and parole violators were returned to prison. As a result, California's corrections populations skyrocketed. (1994, 165)

The modern return of for-profit prisons, then, is driven by several forces operating in unison. First and foremost, the above-illustrated increase in the incarceration rate itself (despite no corresponding increase in crime) contributed dramatically to prison overcrowding. Second, a corresponding increase in the average length of prison sentences for nonviolent drug crime exacerbated prison overcrowding all the more. Combined together, higher incarceration rates and longer sentences dramatically increased costs to taxpayers. Included in these expenses are the substantial costs of new prison construction (as discussed in Chapter 4) and the expanded use of diversionary programs such as boot camps and intensive probation supervision to cope with the overflow (RAND, 1997; Duffee & McGarrell, 1990; Petersilia, 1994; McCarthy, 1987). According to Petersilia, by the early 1990s spending on prison construction in California outpaced spending on education (1994). Finally, as criminologist Michael Tonry writes in his book *Malign Neglect: Race, Crime, and Punishment in America* (in profound consonance with the words of James Baldwin above):

> Although disadvantaged young people of all races and ethnicities have been affected by the drug wars, the greatest attention has been on Hispanics and blacks. Black Americans in particular have been caught, and because of the heavy burdens borne by the war's black victims . . . [in this book] I show why the war's architects should be held accountable for what they have done to damage young black Americans. (1995, pp. 82–85)

Tonry further notes that national rates of black versus white imprisonment, while already showing profound disparity, *underrepresent* concentrations of African American versus white prisoners taken from inner cities. Tonry cites studies documenting that "23 percent of black males aged 20 to 29 were under system control" in New York in 1990, "33 percent of black males aged 20–29" in California in 1990, "42 percent of black males aged 18 to 35" in 1991 Washington, D.C., and, finally, "56 percent of 18-to-35 year old black males in 1991 Baltimore" (pp. 29–30; see Chapter 1).

Thus, in order to understand the true dimensions of the racialized mass incarceration of the current era, it is necessary not only to look at national-level aggregate data but also to look beyond these (already shocking) statistics to examine the rate of incarceration from its primary source: our inner cities—where the effects of social disorganization, alienation, addiction, and familial entropy organize social life.

Supply and Demand: Prison Overcrowding as Good Business

As a result of the swift increase in the use of incarceration, by the early 1990s prisons themselves became overcrowded and dangerous, with roughly two-thirds of U.S. correctional facilities being placed under federal court orders to reduce overcrowding for violations of inmates' Eighth Amendment protection against cruel and unusual punishment (Bohm & Haley, 1997, p. 327). A key consequence of overcrowding is a higher prevalence of violence and injury to inmates and staff, as well as higher use of disciplinary "good time" revocation and higher rates of staff turnover (Silberman, 1995). As overcrowding-related problems increased, the option of trying to relieve its pressures through the use of private prison facilities became even more attractive. Indeed, as explained in Chapter 4, the world's largest (ever) private prison corporation, Corrections Corporation of America, was for all intents and purposes *founded* during a forced special session of the Tennessee legislature called to cope with a prison crisis. As noted in Chapter 2, this was not the first time a prison crisis impacting mostly African Americans coincided with the mercantile solution of privatization: prison overcrowding and the costs associated with "controlling negro crime" were also a rationale of the Convict Lease system (Lichtenstein, 1996, p. 29).

Although "cost savings" is perhaps the most frequent label used to justify prison privatization to the public today, overcrowded prisons created by drug war policies actually created a market opportunity: high demand and low supply. In a classic supply-and-demand business proposal, entrepreneurs sought to meet what they knew would be a steady and increasing demand: incarceration rates and sentence durations were up, whereas supply of prison bed space was limited. According to a 1998 survey of state and federal correctional administrators conducted by Abt Associates, Inc., reducing overcrowding has been and remains, in fact, the primary crisis faced by administrators adopting privatization. Without question, private contractors are consistently able to build large prisons more quickly than any state or the federal government. The report ranks the objectives of prison administrators in regards to privatization in the following order (p. 16):

1. Reducing overcrowding   (86 percent)
2. Speed of acquiring additional beds   (75 percent)
3. Gaining operational flexibility   (61 percent)
4. Construction cost savings   (57 percent)
5. Improving caliber of services   (43 percent)
6. Reducing legal liability exposure   (39 percent)
7. Other   (21 percent)

Current Use of Private Prisons

According to the U.S. Department of Justice *Sourcebook of Criminal Justice Statistics*, as of December 31, 2000, there were fourteen private contractors operating adult correctional facilities in the United States, with a total bed-space capacity of approximately 119,000 (Table 6.1) (Maguire & Pastore, 2002, p. 86). The two largest of these, Corrections Corporation of America and Wackenhut Corrections Corporation, together held roughly 74 percent of the total U.S. prisoners housed in private facilities. It is also worth noting that CCA currently dominates the prison privatization market, holding roughly 52 percent of the privatized inmates, while Wackenhut holds roughly 22 percent (Abt Associates, Inc., 1998, p. 18). The vast majority of these inmates were low security status inmates with nonviolent histories. At the end of 1997, in fact, only one private prison facility in operation was designated exclusively for "maximum security" inmates, the South Bay Correctional Facility in Florida operated by Wackenhut (p. 25).

Themes in Today's Debate about Prison Privatization

The Cost Conundrum

Certainly, a most significant issue regarding prison privatization to be resolved in this century is the issue of whether private prisons can be operated *more cheaply* than state prisons while still achieving comparable performance. Although there are situations in which the evidence suggests that private prisons spend less money than state-operated pris-

Table 6.1 2001 Private Adult Correctional Management Firms and Capacities.

Management firm	Prisoner capacity, Sept. 4, 2001
Alternative Programs, Inc.	340
Avalon Correctional Services	710
Bobby Ross Group	464
CiviGenics, Inc.	2,243
Cornell Corrections, Inc.	8,424
Correctional Services Corp.	3,891
Correctional Systems, Inc.	272
Corrections Corporation of America	62,231
Dominion Correctional Services, Inc.	2,064
GRW Corporation	614
Management and Training Corporation	10,566
Marantha Production Company	500
U.S. Corrections Corporation	N.A.
Wackenhut Corrections Corporation	26,704

ons, the data are not uniform across the sites, and generalizations cannot be made across any jurisdiction or region of the country (Shichor, 1995, p. 136; see also Thomas, 1996). "Determining whether and how privatization saves the government money is difficult in many jurisdictions because no publicly managed prisons exist that are similar enough to warrant direct comparison with private facilities" (Abt Associates, Inc., 1998, p. 34). Thus, in the few cases when privatized facilities are found to be more cost-effective, the salient questions are why and under what conditions (Camp & Gaes, 2002)?

Because an essential argument in favor of prison privatization is that private vendors can provide "more for less," clearly some explanation is in order regarding exactly how private vendors might accomplish this goal (Shichor, 1995). Even though cost savings are not listed by most correctional administrations as being the most important rationale for utilizing private contractors, clearly cost-effectiveness remains one of the central arguments considered by legislators. As privatization proponent and scholar Charles Logan notes, "Among claims made for the superiority of propriety [private] prisons, the most frequent and most salient . . . is that they will be less expensive, or at least more efficient" (1990, p. 76).

The financial stakes in this debate are enormous. In California, for example, corrections has become the fastest-growing state budget category since the mid-1980s—and by the mid-1990s outpaced spending on education—rendering enormous chunks of the state budget available to private prison vendors for the delivery of correctional services (Petersilia, 1994). In recent years, the Ohio Department of Rehabilitation and Corrections has held the largest budget in the state government (Hallett & Hanauer, 2001). Not surprisingly, then, stakeholders on both sides of the privatization debate cling to reports that each finds favorable.

Calculating costs for operating private prison systems across jurisdictions is a very complex matter—requiring a conflation of comparison costs between facilities often differing by jurisdiction, type of inmate, inmate programming and service assignments, salaries of line and administrative staff, overall number of staff, and health care commitments for inmates, for example. This often results in an "apples and oranges" kind of comparison that critics argue renders comparisons between facilities neither valid nor reliable (Camp & Gaes, 2002; Shichor, 1995; U.S. General Accounting Office, 1996). Prison facilities often also differ in "reputation," which, though a somewhat qualitative variable, may dramatically influence operational life inside a prison (Silberman, 1995). The two primary claims about the cost utility of private prisons, however, are clear (see Shichor, 1995): private contractors can operate prisons more cheaply and efficiently than state-based providers, resulting in cost savings for taxpayers, and the quality of services provided by private vendors will be greater than or equal to those provided by state-based providers.

The first difficulty often articulated regarding making valid and reliable cost assessments of performance between public and private correctional facilities is that costs are a highly regional phenomenon. Thus, when comparing costs it is vital that the comparisons be made between as nearly similar institutions as possible, in as nearly similar regions as possible (Thomas, 1996, p. 12n20; U.S. General Accounting Office, 1996, p. 5). It would be patently unfair, for example, to compare the costs of operating a prison in the rural South to the costs of operating a prison in Houston, Texas, or California—as this would greatly distort the averages. As Abt Associates's 1998 detailed analysis of privatization further notes about cost evaluations between public and private prisons:

> The task of selecting fully comparable prisons is difficult, if not impossible. Differences in the age, health, gender, and security risk of inmates would imply differences in the reported cost per inmate-day even among equally efficient prison facilities. The same may be said for differences in the size of the inmate population and regional differences in the cost of labor and materials. One could use regression analysis to "correct" for these differences if there were a large enough number of roughly comparable prisons in a given system. In the absence of such data, the only available alternative is to adjust on a case-by-case basis. Not surprisingly, this approach leaves room for considerable disagreement over the appropriate scale of the adjustment factors. (1998, app. 1n7)

Where savings from prison privatization have been demonstrated, they are consistently derived from a narrow set of sources: hiring fewer staff with lower benefits, choosing to serve mostly minimum- and medium-security inmates who are healthy, and operating in relatively newer facilities with more efficient designs and newer equipment (Camp & Gaes, 2002). The greatest level of savings, however, is achieved in staffing-related expenses. "Prisons are extremely labor-intensive, with approximately 65 to 70 percent of the costs of operating a prison related to staff salaries, fringe benefits, and overtime" (Austin & Irwin, 2001, p. 73). As privatization proponent Charles Thomas notes, "It is generally acknowledged that private-sector fringe benefits—most particularly retirement benefits—are less generous than those made available to public employees" (1996, p. 10).

The 1996 U.S. General Accounting Office report on prison privatization and cost is often cited as the most reliable study on the topic (see Abt Associates, Inc., 1998, p. 37). It closely examined five studies in California, Texas, Washington, Tennessee, and New Mexico, analyzing both operational costs and quality of service.

> These studies offer little generalizable guidance for other jurisdictions about what to expect regarding comparative operational costs and quality of service if they were to move toward privatizing correctional facilities. First, several of the studies focused on specialized inmate populations, such as those in pre-release situations, that limited their generalizability to a wider inmate population. Second, methodological weaknesses in some of the comparisons—such as using hypothetical facilities or non-random survey samples—make some findings questionable, even for the study setting. Third, a variety of differences in other states and regions could result in experiences far different from those of the states that were studied. For example, cost of living and a state's correctional philosophy could affect the comparative costs and quality of private and public facilities from state to state. Finally, the age or maturity of the private system could affect the relationship between private and public facilities in terms of costs and quality. (1996, p. 4)

An additional cost issue raised by evaluators of private prisons is that for-profit prison operations may be inclined to cut costs too much, resulting in a decreased level of service and safety for communities, inmates, and staff in and around correctional facilities that are privatized. James Austin and John Irwin's survey of private prisons revealed that "the number of staff assigned to private facilities per inmate population is approximately 15 percent lower than at public facilities," raising questions about costs versus safety (2001, p. 83). Indeed, as recently noted, a Tennessee legislative report from the state's Select Oversight Committee on Corrections, comparing public and private correctional facilities, stated:

> The number of injuries to staff and prisoners is a measure of the security and safety of the facility. During the fifteen-month evaluation period, South Central Correctional Center [the privately operated facility] reported

significantly more injuries to prisoners and staff than either Northeast Correctional Center or Northwest Correctional Center *[both operated by the state]*, with 214 injuries reported at SCCC, 21 and 51 at Northeast Correctional Center and Northwest Correctional Center, respectively. The use of force is also reviewed when looking at the security and safety of a prison. The facilities have significantly different reported incidents of the use of force. South Central Correctional Center had 30 reported incidents, Northeast Correctional Center 4, and Northwest Correctional Center 6. (1995, p. vii, as cited in Hallett & Lee, 2000, p. 234; bracketed text in italics added for clarity)

Thus, assessing the true costs (and benefits) of private prisons is a very complex and politically volatile process. With the promise of jobs, communities are often eager to consider privatization proposals (Harden, 2002; see also Chapter 5).

Caveat Emptor: "Hidden Costs"

One of the key difficulties involved in accurately calculating the true cost of a correctional operation has to do with so-called hidden costs. The term "does not imply that [costs] are deliberately concealed, only that they are not easily discernible" (Logan & McGriff, 1989, p. 2). Hidden costs include expenses that involve unforeseen events, such as expenditures related to unexpected medical conditions, escapes, or unplanned damage to a facility. Because budgetary forecasting is generally done by singular institutional agencies, hidden costs usually first reveal themselves in cross-agency budget analyses when combined costs are more evident. As Charles Logan and Bill W. McGriff note, "Costs omitted from [single-agency] correctional budgets can amount to one-third the value of those that are included" (ibid.). One of the key problems in forecasting costs in private for-profit prisons is the continuous reality that unexpected things often happen in prisons. Although per diem costs and services are relatively fixed, "unexpected" costs can be fairly substantial (Shichor, 1995). For example, in the aftermath of several high-profile escapes from CCA-operated prisons in Youngstown, Ohio, and Clifton, Tennessee, local jurisdictions paid for the expenses related to recapturing the escaped inmates. These costs, of course, have to then be added to the total cost of operating the private facility paid by the contracting jurisdiction. Moreover, "Some of the apparent differences may not reflect actual savings but may instead be accounting artifacts . . . because public and private accounting systems are designed for different purposes; that is, public systems were not designed specifically for cost accounting (Abt Associates, Inc., 1998, p. iv). With the Enron scandal of recent vintage, these considerations become important.

A recent story in the *Wall Street Journal* documents Arthur Andersen's "off the books financing" for public and private operators of prisons. The private corrections firm Cornell Corrections Corporation, for example, recently sought to create a subsidiary company called Municipal Corrections to which it would shift all of its debt on paper, for a fee, thus making Cornell itself look more profitable. This debt transfer was partly underwritten by Lehman's Financing Corporation. According to the *Wall Street Journal*, this arrangement helped drive Cornell's stock "to new highs." "In return for helping to cleanse *Cornell*'s debt, Lehman and Provident expected rewards. Lehman is to collect a $2 million fee for selling the bonds, according to the deal documents." Such off-the-books financing deals have been arranged for states as well, such as North Carolina. "North Carolina wanted more cells but sought to finance them off of its own books. It invited bids from contractors willing to borrow the money for construction" (Hallinan, 2002; on such financing of private prison firms, see Chapter 5).

In sum, the few highly detailed studies on the cost-effectiveness of private prisons available have failed to offer compelling evidence of savings produced by private prisons. Part of the problem in demonstrating cost savings for private prisons is that the overall scale of prison privatization remains small, and it is difficult to ensure that private versus public institutions are dealing with the same types of inmates. As Austin and Irwin point out, currently the percentage of inmates held in private facilities is well under 10 percent in every state. Assuming that private prison facilities could achieve a 10 percent cost savings (far above what they have actually been shown to save) for 10 percent of a given state's inmates, the resulting savings would still be a net savings of only 1 percent systemwide (2001, p. 73). Moreover, in the relatively few evaluation studies designed to control for differences in public versus private accounting systems, inmate population differences, and staffing levels, the data remain inconclusive for the cost-effectiveness of private prisons. The Abt Associates report finds:

> Our conclusion regarding costs and savings is that the few existing studies and other available data do not provide strong evidence of any general pattern. Some states may be willing to pay high prices for private impris-

onment if they need the beds to solve short-term deficiencies. In other states, expenditures for contracting may indeed be lower than for direct public provision. However, the bottom line with respect to savings is difficult to discern given the data and the assumptions made by analysts. Drawing conclusions about the inherent superiority of one or the other mode of provision, based on a few studies, is premature. (1998, p. v)

"Creaming," "Skimming," and "Cherry Picking"

As noted in Chapter 2, during the operation of the Convict Lease system private contractors developed a classification system based on an inmate's productivity and ability to work. Convicts were literally divided into three classes of workers and valued accordingly. In today's private prison market, the vast majority of which is concentrated on minimum-security inmates, a classification system of sorts is in place as well. In this case, however, private companies prefer the most docile of inmates rather than the most vigorous. As noted corrections researchers Todd Clear and George F. Cole point out: "Most privatization plans call for skimming off the best of the worst—the non-serious offenders who can be efficiently processed. Thus the government-run part of the correctional system faces the possibility of having to manage only the most costly, most intractable offenders on a reduced budget, and with the worsened fiscal and personnel situations that would result from such a development" (1994, p. 513).

"Creaming," "skimming," or "cherry picking," then, refers to the practice of private corporations contracting primarily for those inmates in the prisoner population that are the easiest to deal with and the cheapest to manage (ibid.; Bureau of Justice Statistics, 1996). Prisoners who have violent tendencies or who have communicable diseases such as AIDS, for example, are traditionally shunned by private industry contractors. Put another way, "creaming" refers to the practice of taking the "best" offenders available in a population for the contract of private services—like counseling and drug or alcohol treatment—in order to yield the highest profits. Because many *public* facilities are required by law to deal with a broader spectrum of inmates, achieving accurate comparisons to the performance of privately run facilities becomes problematic (see Camp & Gaes, 2002). Finally, in Florida, Bales et al. found "no empirical justification for the policy argument that private prisons reduce recidivism better than public prisons (Bales, Bedard, Quinn, Ensley, & Holley, 2005, p. 57).

Free Market "Competition" (Benefits) versus Service-Provider
Captivity (Risks)

Many commentators on prison privatization have issued warnings against
the possibility of jurisdictions becoming "captive" to prison service vendors (Bowditch & Everett, 1991; Shichor, 1995; Walzer, 1991). That is,
once a jurisdiction delegates its authority to manage and operate a correctional facility to a private corporation, the jurisdiction also runs the risk
of becoming overly dependent upon that corporation for services. Because
only two corporations are, frankly, large and experienced enough to handle most large-scale prison privatization contracts, CCA and Wackenhut
(now Group 4 Securicor), and given the fact that the U.S. Department of
Justice recommends using only experienced and capable private prison
corporations for such contracts, a question emerges about how much
"choice" a jurisdiction actually has—especially in the event it wishes
to *terminate* a service contract with a private prison corporation once
underwritten.[1]

In an ideal free-market system, numerous providers exist to serve
customers' needs—and customers enforce efficiency by virtue of their
option to cease transacting with one provider in favor of another. In conditions where competition among vendors is limited, however, so too
are customers' options. So, for example, in a case where only a limited
number of private prison vendors are large or experienced enough to
handle a multilevel (minimum, medium, and maximum security) inmate
population, then clearly the benefits of the free-market system become
less powerful.

One of the key justifications for privatization put forward by its proponents is that private contractors operate more efficiently than their
public-sector counterparts because they are subject to the forces of competition. Proponents argue that because state-based service providers are
often locked into contracts with other state or local service agencies,
there is much less flexibility available to governmental jurisdictions
in managing the facilities (Logan, 1990; Fitzgerald, 1991). This "lack of
flexibility" is put forward as a source of governmental inefficiency and
excessive cost to taxpayers, because governmental bureaucracies have
no incentive to downsize. Privatization proponents argue that private
contractors have no such allegiances and are not bound by similar procurement rules, thus being able to "shop around" for competitive prices
and workers.

Two issues have emerged regarding the claimed benefits of "competition" in the context of for-profit prisons, however: truly competitive bidding is often not realized (or required) in the contracting process, and the private prison industry is itself dominated by two major providers—Corrections Corporation of America and Wackenhut Corrections Corporation[2]—thus limiting the operational amount of true competition in the industry itself (Bureau of Justice Statistics, 1996). In 1997 in Tennessee, for example, the state legislature gave serious consideration to awarding CCA a contract for operating the state's *entire* prison system—despite a consultant's recommendation that they parcel out the contracts among several companies, in order to instill true competition (Hallett & Lee, 2000). As prison privatization researcher David Shichor notes: "When private companies hold monopolies, they also lose their efficiency and flexibility, like in the cost of public utilities" (1995, p. 17).

The "captivity" danger, then, is this: because private vendors like Wackenhut and CCA have become so large—and because one of the key criteria in the awarding of contracts is a "demonstrated ability to handle populations like those under consideration"—they have a competitive advantage in contract bidding of all kinds (National Institute of Justice, 1987, p. 33). Evidence of the monopolistic power that private prison corporations have acquired was recently demonstrated by the remarks of CCA spokeswoman Peggy Lawrence and CCA president Doctor Crants, after losing two separate service contracts, one with the State of South Carolina and the other with Washington, D.C.: "The government needs us to stay in that business," and "The fact of the matter is that D.C. needs us more than we need D.C." ("CCA Deal Breakdown," 1997).

Finally, the possibility of bankruptcy must be considered and accounted for in any contract for private prison services (National Institute of Justice, 1987). Should a private contractor find itself out of business, short of cash, or unable to deliver the level of service required (the latter happened to CCA in a South Carolina facility), then the state would be liable for resuming its stewardship of the state prisons ("CCA Deal Breakdown," 1997). This is problematic because it leaves governmental jurisdictions in the position of having to reallocate commitments, with any money saved by privatization put back into its corrections functions. In addition, numerous commentators have noted that the likely transition costs of the state moving back in to take control of a privatized facility could be considerable (Robbins, 1998). Privatization researchers have now suggested that separate insurance policies be taken out by jurisdictions to guard against private vendor bankruptcy and that they must be factored into the cost assessment of privatization contracts (Gilbert, 2000b).

Contract and Monitoring Issues

Because the state is delegating its authority to govern the lives and freedom of the inmates it sends to a private corporation, and because life in prison takes place well outside of public view, it is necessary for the state to closely monitor the level of service provided by contractors. "The function of monitoring is to ensure that the private operator is in compliance with the provisions of the contract" (Shichor, 1995, p. 119). Independent evaluation of the performance of privatized facilities is vital for both contract enforcement as well as a thorough accounting of the merits and deficiencies of prison privatization generally. It is important to note the difference between "monitoring" and "evaluation." *Monitoring* refers to the continuous examination of the level of service provided by vendors. *Evaluation* refers to a broader, more impact-based set of criteria that may include issues of monitoring but extend beyond them to an examination of the efficacy of private prisons as a whole.

A central concern in the area of monitoring is the expense involved—especially because the nature of the monitoring required for a privatized prison goes well beyond those of ensuring cost compliance. A special effort must be made on the part of the state to ensure that daily life inside the prison is under way within legal bounds. Thus, "monitoring is intended to ascertain that prisoners are securely incarcerated (thus protecting the public and penalizing those breaking the law), that the inmates themselves are being adequately treated (without violating their rights or providing unreasonable punishment), and that reasonable rehabilitation efforts are being provided" (NIJ, 1987, p. 47). Needless to say, this can be quite an involved undertaking. The National Institute of Justice notes the following about the State of Pennsylvania's monitoring plan: "The State of Pennsylvania's Legislative Budget and Finance Committee in its October 1985 report stated that the law should designate a specific agency as responsible for monitoring private prisons; this process should include periodic [on-site] inspections, evaluations, and specification of minimum standards" (1987, p. 47). Privatization researcher Charles Logan emphasizes the merits of outside monitoring: "Here, the point is that independent monitoring promotes objectivity and rigor in the overall supervision of a prison. It is easier to be consistent when imposing standards of outsiders than when enforcing them on ourselves or our colleagues" (1990, p. 207). The National Institute of Justice, however, notes that "there are two disadvantages of on-site monitoring. First, it is expensive to maintain the monitor and provide the required resources such as secretarial support, telephone, equipment, and materials. . . . The second problem with the on-site monitoring is the possibility that the monitor would be co-opted by the contractor's staff" (1987, p. 49). In sum, intensive monitoring is a costly—but necessary—part of any privatization undertaking.

High Turnover

A key and related issue for corrections is its continuously high turnover of staff. In fact, corrections, more than any other criminal justice profession, has the highest rate of turnover (Cole, 1994). High turnover leads to instability within the institution and the corresponding administrative need for continual recruitment and training. This results in a disproportionate number of inexperienced and untrained staff.

Reasons for the high turnover rate in corrections are numerous. First, corrections tends to be a fairly low-paying field, with comparatively modest benefits. Second, corrections is often very dangerous work exacting a high level of work-related stress. Finally, another key reason is the relatively meager opportunity for professional advancement (ibid.). Taken together, these factors can lead to problems with staff morale, tardiness and absenteeism, and a general state of turmoil (Clear & Cole, 1994). In the context of privatized prisons, these problems have all been documented and may be worse than those in the public sector, as articulated by Alan M. Schuman, the director of the Social Service Division in the Washington, D.C., Superior Court:

> Privately financed institutions can cut costs by paying lower salaries and can reduce costs even further by providing no or minimum pension and fringe benefit packages. However, lower salaries could attract less qualified staff who would require extensive high quality training, and this would offset some of the cost savings. My personal observation has been that privately funded agencies offer lower salaries and have very high staff turnover rates. In fact, many of the best qualified private sector staff eventually apply for public sector probation positions that offer more job security and higher salaries. The high turnover rate must impact the quality of services that are provided; a factor that should be considered in any cost analysis formula. (quoted in Shichor, 1995, p. 194)

Finally, Scott D. Camp and Gerald G. Gaes (2002) found staff turnover to be a widespread problem among private prison facilities nationwide.

Legal Issues

One prevailing legal issue involved in privatization has revolved around the extent to which a state may constitutionally delegate its authority to punish. Specifically, legal questions surrounding the ability of a state to delegate its authority to make punishment decisions—and the liability associated with having made them—has been taking center stage in the legal debate over prison privatization. As David Shichor notes: "Many critics and even supporters agree that when a government deprives its citizens of their liberty, it exercises state power" (1995, p. 52). Thus, some of the central legal issues regarding privatizing prisons involve *the delegation of the state's authority* to use force or make forceful decisions that have consequences for inmates. In perhaps the most significant legal development on the privatization front in recent years, the United States Supreme Court recently ruled in *Richardson v. McKnight* (1997) that guards at a privately run prison facility in Clifton, Tennessee, are not entitled to the same level of immunity from liability that state guards are sometimes afforded. Stated Justice Stephen Breyer for the Court: "Our examination of the history and purpose of the industry . . . reveals nothing special enough about the job or about its organizational structure that would warrant providing these prison guards with a governmental immunity." In his written opinion, Justice Antonin Scalia also noted that "this decision is sure to artificially raise the cost of privatizing prisons. Whether this will cause privatization to be prohibitively expensive, or instead simply divert state funds that could have been saved or spent on additional prison services, it is likely that taxpayers and prisoners will suffer as a consequence" ("CCA Loses," 1997).

The legal questions surrounding prison privatization, however, involve more than just the issue of whether a privately paid guard can use force against an inmate as a delegate of the state, but also whether representatives of a private company may engage in behavior or decision making (for example, writing disciplinary reports or revoking privileges) that has any detrimental effect upon an inmate whatsoever. A prevailing concern here is that privately paid guards—directly supervised by company, not state, representatives—owe primary allegiance to the company but act "under color of law" on behalf of the state. Other questions regarding the accessibility that privately held inmates have to legal materials and due-process issues surrounding the interstate transfer of inmates are working their way through the courts at this writing. Inmates housed in out-of-state prisons for the purposes of saving states' money, for example, may face difficulties in accessing their local attorneys or in staying connected with family members.

Related constitutional questions impacting for-profit imprisonment have to do with the constitutionality of so-called mandatory-sentencing policies such as California's "three strikes and you're out" legislation. This legislation, also sometimes referred to as "habitual offender" legislation, provides for lengthy—even lifetime—incarceration of offenders deemed to be "chronic" offenders, even upon conviction for minor crimes. Such legislation has produced controversial sentences, for example, of twenty-five years to life for petty theft. In California, the state with the nation's highest incarceration rate, "of the 7,300 prisoners sentenced to 25 years to life, more than 2,000 are behind bars for burglary or theft and some 700 for drug possession." Some of the other theft charges associated with twenty five-to-life sentences include shoplifting of a $20 bottle of vitamins and a $3 magazine (Roosevelt, 2004, p. 38). In March 2003, the Supreme Court of the United States upheld the constitutionality of the three-strikes law in a narrow five-to-four decision. Among the cases involved in the Supreme Court's deliberation was the upholding of a fifty-to-life sentence for theft of $153 in videotapes (Egelko, 2004). At the time of the ruling, Reverend Jesse Jackson issued the following statement in the *Chicago Sun-Times:*

> The court was blind not only to elemental justice, but to common sense as well. Across the country, these absurd laws have tied the hands of judges, and forced long sentences for hundreds of thousands of inmates for nonviolent crimes. With racial profiling by police, entrenched prosecutorial bias and often stacked juries, the victims of these injustices are overwhelmingly minorities—African American and Latino—and male. With a staggering 2 million people incarcerated, the prison-industrial complex has become a big industry. Small communities, starved for jobs, compete to host a prison. Small businesses, starved for contracts, compete to privatize parts or the whole, hoping to reap a profit from others' misery. (Jackson, 2003)

Finally, although the U.S.A. Patriot Act has been the subject of much debate by civil libertarians, the legislative crackdown on illegal immigrants began well before September 11, 2001, in the United States. "While recent observations on the government's crackdown on illegal immigrants in a post 9/11 society suggest that this is a new phenomenon, evidence to the contrary clearly demonstrates that punitive immigration policies were in full swing before the events of September 11th, 2001" (Welch, 2005, p. 3). Specifically, the 1996 Illegal Immigration Reform and Immigrant Responsibility Act and the 1996 Antiterrorism and Effective Death Penalty Act have helped redefine immigrants and how they are seen in American society. The Illegal Immigration Reform and Immigrant Responsibility Act defined immigrants as criminals and vagrants in search of welfare benefits. "Whereas previous immigration laws were formulated according to such concerns as skilled labor and family-reunification, legislation passed in 1996 was shaped by a tendency to criminalize immigrants" (p. 6).

Construction Costs of Prison Facilities

The available evidence on the cost-effectiveness of privatized *construction* of prison facilities strongly suggests that there are indeed significant cost savings produced when private companies contract with jurisdictional entities to *build* a prison facility (Thomas, 1996; Shichor, 1995). The reasons for this are numerous: First, private corporations are not bound by existing state contracts with suppliers and can "shop around" in their acquisition of building materials. Second, private companies are able to avoid the need to comply with governmental oversight in contract allocation and decision making, thus saving time. Third, private contractors are free from the sometimes-lengthy approval process in procurement, enabling private corporations to more efficiently purchase and deliver necessary materials to remote prison construction sites (Thomas, 1996; Fitzgerald, 1991). As mentioned above, however, state and local governments commonly look to private financial concerns to assist in the financing of prison construction—which enables the construction to proceed without having to put the issue before voters in the form of a referendum. Jurisdictions simply contract with the financier (for a fee, of course) to assemble the necessary capital for prison construction. This enables politicians to avoid the criticism of "expanding the size of government," as prisons surely do, without having to get voter approval for doing so.

Moral, Racial, and Ethical Issues

Clearly, the overriding moral and ethical issue surrounding the emergence of for-profit prisons is the fact that the industry's stock-in-trade is human beings: the more people locked up, the more profitable the industry. Though some fear that this new incentive for incarceration puts the traditional criminological goal of reducing crime in danger (Garland, 2001a), it is also clearly the case that the era of mass incarceration has produced large populations of dispossessed people who become the basis of profit for others. Although prison overcrowding was a primary rationale used for the adoption of private prisons in 1980s America, concern about overcrowding soon became displaced by the potential economic benefits of private prisons—as a tool for local economic development. Indeed, from the perspective of a privatized *market* in incarceration, overcrowded or filled-to-capacity prisons are a good thing: *as overcrowding goes up, costs go down*. Finally, the *racial* disparities prevalent in today's for-profit prison system in America disturbingly match those established at the time of the Convict Lease system. As larger and larger populations of human beings come to be viewed as elements of a for-profit imprisonment plan, real questions about social justice and citizenship itself need to be examined.

There are other questions as well. As recently documented in Tennessee, Corrections Corporation of America widely donated campaign monies to proprivatization candidates (Hallett & Lee, 2000; see Chapter 4). Though no ethical breach is automatic, many argue that even the appearance of such a connection between policy and politics is cause for concern (Shichor, 1995; Ethridge & Marquart, 1993, p. 38).

One final ethical issue bears mentioning. Although in the United States it is clear that criminal justice policy has moved away from the ethic of rehabilitation in favor of an ethic of punishment, it is also certain that the experiences of prisoners while they are in prison are powerful determinants of their behavior after release (Silberman, 1995; Sabol, 2002). Given the concerns about the elevated level of violence and the documented problems of for-profit corporations in charge of feeding inmates and providing health care, questions emerge about the potential long-lasting and negative impacts that cheaply run for-profit prisons can have regardless of the short-term cost savings. Just close your eyes and think this through: What does it mean to have a *for-profit* prison system? What does it mean for democracy? What does it mean for social equality? What does it mean for the future of the country? What does it mean for the present?

SEVEN

Commerce with Criminals: The New Colonialism in Criminal Justice

> The overweening, defining event of the modern world is the mass movement of raced populations, beginning with the largest forced transfer of people in the history of the world: slavery. The consequences of which transfer have determined all the wars following it as well as the current ones being waged on every continent. The contemporary world's work has become policing, halting, forming policy regarding, and trying to administer the movement of people. Nationhood—the very definition of citizenship—is constantly being demarcated and redemarcated in response to exiles, refugees, Gastarbeiter, immigrants, migrations, the displaced, the fleeing, and the besieged.
>
> —Toni Morrison, "Home"

Race, Colonialism, and the Rise of Penology: Penal Commerce in Laborers

In his biography of Thomas Jefferson, Willard Sterne Randall thoroughly documents Jefferson's public aversion to slavery; his blaming of the British Crown for chartering the "world's leading slave trader," the Royal African Company in 1660; and his continued reliance upon slaves in his private affairs (1993, p. 143).

Private commerce with prisoners has been under way for centuries in Anglo societies, dating back to the 1600s. This commerce involved the prospective use of captives' labor to expand the colonial power of Great Britain at virtually no cost to the state, while also providing a mechanism for exile of the "dangerous classes" (Shelden, 2001). Privatized mechanisms for processing adjudicated offenders, therefore, have long been a routinized form of criminal justice activity. To a remarkable degree, this mercantile system of offender management has been developed not by state officials, but by commercial entrepreneurs dependent upon criminal adjudication for their profits (Feeley, 2002). Transportation, a practice developed by private merchant shippers in seventeenth-century England, literally involved "transporting" convicted criminals to North American and Australian plantations for periods of indentured labor (Hughes, 1987).

This "privatized" sentencing option cheaply expanded the sanctioning power of the state and exponentially increased the case-processing capacity of the criminal justice system (Feeley, 2002). Later, free indentured servants—generally for the cost of passage—submitted "voluntarily" to transportation and a period of indenture from four to seven years, in exchange for being pardoned for such petty crimes as vagrancy (Smith, 1965, pp. 89–135). "Actual shipment of the convicts was performed by merchants trading to the plantations. . . . The merchants made their profit by selling the convicts as indentured servants in the colonies" (pp. 97–98). The epigraph to Robert Hughes's masterpiece history of transportation and Australia's founding, *The Fatal Shore* (1987), invokes a convict ballad:

> The very day we landed upon the Fatal Shore,
> The planters stood around us, full twenty score or more;
> They ranked us up like horses and sold us out of hand,
> They chained us up to pull the plow, upon Van Diemen's Land.

Without question, then, one of the key forces driving the historical practice of commerce with criminals in America was British colonial imperialism. In the case of transportation, colonial use of convict laborers was thought a commonsensical solution to the problems of crime and listlessness in Great Britain, as well as a useful means of expanding British influence abroad at no expense to the Crown. White indentured servants during this period, however, were keenly distinguished from

"Negro slaves." People subject to these differing forms of servitude "were variously known as indentured servants, redemptioners, or, in order to distinguish them from the Negroes, as Christian or white servants" (Smith, 1965, p. 3).

The abolition of transportation, however, exacerbated the utility of slavery in colonial America, where "society was not democratic and certainly not equalitarian" (p. 7). Agricultural production mechanisms of the time were labor intensive, requiring large numbers of slaves to till, plant, harvest, process, transport, and refine products. The racist doctrine of "white supremacy" conveniently began to thrive during this period, with the exploitation-derived benefits of the African slave trade quickly surpassing those of white indentured servitude (ibid.). Slaves, after all, had no right to ultimate freedom.

Labor and Confinement: The Racial History of For-Profit Imprisonment in the United States

The demise of transportation left Great Britain with the need for an alternative mechanism through which to manage large numbers of prisoners. The privately managed prison was presented by Jeremy Bentham as a reasonable option. In a consummately insightful sales pitch, Bentham remarks on the utility of captivity for enhancing labor productivity: "What hold can any other manufacturer have upon his workmen, equal to what my manufacturer would have upon his? What other master is there that can reduce his workmen, if idle, to a situation next to starving, without suffering them to go elsewhere?" (Bozovic, 1995, p. 71). The answer, of course, as the former British colony well understood, was slavery itself: escape was nearly impossible and punishable by death.

It is perhaps astonishing to realize that the very instrument of slavery's abolition in the United States, the Thirteenth Amendment to the U.S. Constitution—also authorized the "involuntary servitude" of prisoners as a punishment for crime. During the operation of the Convict Lease system, from 1865 to the 1920s, the Thirteenth Amendment simultaneously enabled the continuation of racialized forced labor in the South at what was supposed to be the start of freedom for African American slaves. Upon release from their former owners' captivity, "emancipated" slaves often had nowhere to go—and found themselves designated trespassers, disturbers of the peace, vagrants, or loiterers on their former owners' plantations (Shelden, 2001, p. 170). Caught between the legal restrictions of abolition and a paramount need for cheap labor, Convict Leasing emerged as a uniquely southern solution to the postbellum labor shortage and facilitated a continuation of the ideology of white supremacy.

Lessons of Prison Privatization: Mass Imprisonment and For-Profit Prisons

As pointed out by Scott Christianson, "Between 1985 and 1995, there was a 500 percent increase in private prisons; 18 companies had rehabilitated 93 private prisons, creating space for some 51,000 prisoners" (1998, p. 291). Today, private prisons constitute the fourth-largest prison system in the country, holding roughly 91,000 inmates, most of whom are racial minorities and the largest single portion of whom are black men.

Many entrepreneurs of for-profit imprisonment remain hopeful about the future. A March 2003 story from Reuters newswire, "Budget Crunch May Help Private Prisons," quotes CCA president John Ferguson as being optimistic about the company's prospects despite a faltering economy: "We believe that existing prison overcrowding, combined with budget difficulties facing many of our customers, should lead to greater demand for our services over the coming years" (James, 2003).

More important, what is revealed by the statements from high-level executives in the private prison industry is a particular *orientation* to the crime problem that is very different from that of the public criminal justice system. Whereas the public system has always tended to view crime and the prevalence of offenders as a costly liability, for-profit entrepreneurs view crime as an economic opportunity and individual criminals as commodities. The reemergence of private prisons in the United States at this particular moment of African American and minority mass imprisonment raises startling questions about the role of race in contemporary criminal justice policy.

Racist History of For-Profit Imprisonment

Throughout the history of the West, but especially in the history of the United States, forsaken people have been people of color—"others," who have little economic or political power. These populations have long been subject to entrepreneurial schemes seeking to "manage" their plight for private profit. As the modern welfare state recedes in political and budgetary importance, private for-profit schemes for managing the dispossessed have returned in the United States, Europe, and Australia as well. In the United States, however, the history of for-profit imprisonment is indelibly tied to African Americans.

Criminology has played right along with the reemergent trend toward privatization, developing research agendas around the "routine activities" of marginal versus well-placed citizens and figuring out ways to better enable the "haves" to avoid coming into contact with "have-nots" through "target hardening" (making people harder to victimize), supplying more capable guardians (hiring more police), and higher incarceration of offenders in for-profit prisons. Such schemes are not new in criminal justice, but date back to the for-profit schemes of Jeremy Bentham himself and the Enlightenment-era notion that the administration of proper doses of pain will deter offenders (a notion contradicted by recent recidivism data, as noted below).

Privatized Ecology of Crime: Social Disorganization as Market Opportunity

Socially disorganized communities often have high rates of criminality due to the fact that the social and human capital available to residents that might help them succeed through legal avenues is limited. Moreover, as public resources are diverted toward prisons and away from programs in education and child care, for example, socially disadvantaged communities struggle all the more. For-profit imprisonment schemes seek to capitalize on this "market" of disfranchised persons who are more likely to end up in prison, less likely to have adequate education, and unlikely to be well represented politically. For-profit imprisonment is big business once again in the United States and is fast becoming a *multinational* industry of inter- and intrastate commerce in human beings not seen since the era of transportation.

Within the United States itself, of course, we also have the for-profit interstate commerce of shipping inmates routinely across state lines for the purpose of obtaining higher per diem payments for their confinement. Meanwhile, the public and academic debate about for-profit imprisonment has been largely dominated by micromanagement issues, rather than by a macrohistorical perspective like that advanced in this book. Although discussion of these topics has taken place, it has been largely confined to "activist" rather than mainstream academic and political circles (Hallett & Lee, 2000; Davis, 1998).

Social Engineering in Postmodern "Twilight Civilization"

> Here are people we are entitled to hate—but only so long as we think of them as victimizers rather than victims.
>
> —Stuart Scheingold, *The Politics of Street Crime: Criminal Process and Cultural Obsession*

Platforms associated with "welfare reform," "charitable choice," and "privatization" emerge in the context of larger things happening in world, namely, the globalization of privately owned and controlled market economies and devolution of public service programs to local governments and private corporations. This prioritization of market-based solutions to public problems corresponds with decreasing state commitments to maintaining social welfare—and are in accord with racially biased criminal justice policies that unfairly target African Americans for political gain. Today we see a convergence of these social welfare and criminal justice policies—under the guise of "privatization," "welfare reform," and "faith-based" prisons. The reemergence of for-profit arrangements of social control in the United States marks a new frontier of literally postmodern social engineering: the "modern" state has given up, ceding its responsibility back to the less democratic stewardship of the (now global) market. The ultimate irony, of course, is that mass imprisonment is hardly an example of "less government."

Punishment assumes a modern, "instrumentalist" social-engineering agenda—one that, as David Garland (1990, 2001a) points out—in modern times has become decidedly antimodern, in that we refuse to acknowledge the mountains of evidence showing that long-term imprisonment does not work. Garland attributes this to a decidedly modern sentiment: "Perhaps what is most in need of explanation is the persistence, since the Enlightenment, of the belief that punishment can work as a positive force for the good of the offender and society, despite the recurring disappointments and sobering experiences of practitioners throughout this whole period" (1990, p. 4n3).

The harshness and corresponding ineffectiveness of our punishment schemes are revealed by the increase in rates of recidivism in the aftermath of our most recent "war" on crime, as revealed by official U.S. Justice Department data. Specifically, these data reveal an increase in recidivism precisely in the aftermath of the period in which we sought to "get tough on crime" (Langan & Levin, 2002). The highest rate of increase in recidivism between 1983 and 1994 was for drug crime (Figure

7.1). Indeed, study after study in criminal justice reveals that "more system" does not equal "less crime," whether it be more police officers or more prisons (Petersilia, 1994).

The death penalty is another good example of how punishment plays a largely *symbolic* rather than functional role in our society: Thurgood Marshall's objections to the death penalty in *Furman v. Georgia* (1972) are instructive here. In addition to the fact that most murderers are not even eligible for the death penalty because their crime is not premeditated:

- the death penalty is biased against poor blacks;
- the costs of execution exceed the costs of life in prison;
- we often condemn the wrong person; and
- the death penalty may actually increase violence.

Statistics showing a very high recidivism rate for our "corrections" system have led many to ask if punishment is really about crime control. Alternatively, does punishment only symbolically deal with crime—while mostly acting as a mechanism for reordering social life along lines of preexisting power (Garland, 1990)? When we declare "wars" on crime, do we do so against corrupt accounting firms that cost thousands of jobs, or do we declare war against the poor, relatively defenseless, uneducated, and already largely condemned "street offender"? All these data beg the

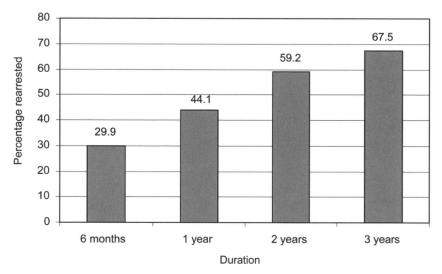

Figure 7.1 Recidivism of U.S. state prisoners released in 1994.

following questions: Why might it be that we declare "wars" against some criminals and not others? What social meanings may we derive from the unequal application of punishment in society? Clearly, such unevenness in punishment reveals that the political act of punishment involves many social motives that extend far beyond "crime control." As Cornel West summarizes these conditions, in regard to our willingness to "privatize" society, we live in a "twilight civilization" today, much more so than in a modern one: "Criminal punishment means hundreds of thousands of black men in crowded prisons—many in there forever. And suburban privatization means black urban poor citizens locked into decrepit public schools, dilapidated housing, inadequate health care and unavailable child care" (1999, p. 116).

Drugs, Crime, Slavery, Profit: The New "Negro" Crime Problem

As documented in Chapter 2, the aftermath of the Civil War saw huge increases in the rate of incarceration of African American men. Criminalized for petty, mostly property, crimes driven by their destitution, "free" black men were incarcerated for lengthy periods and put to work for private profit under the auspices of the Convict Lease system. Legislative changes to statutory punishments were made to increase the penalties for these crimes, thus capturing a large population of available workers for private profit. In much the same way, legislative changes made during the 1980s recategorized crimes committed disproportionately by African Americans as felonies, mandating much longer terms of incarceration for certain drug crimes. In both cases, the changes in law increased penalties for what were formerly nonserious crimes and served interests other than crime control.

In the case of the Convict Lease system, harsher punishments for the large population of "free" but destitute former slaves secured for the devastated agrarian South a captive labor force and a renewed source of white supremacy. In the case of the drug war, harsher punishments for nonviolent drug crimes served the interests of politicians strategically capitalizing on racial tension in American society to get reelected while dismantling the welfare state (Beckett, 1997).

A key strategy in the war on crime was the implementation of a "determinate" or "mandatory minimum" sentencing scheme, which sought both to lengthen the duration of time served by offenders as well as to limit the ability of judges and parole boards to reduce the actual amount of time inmates served (Clear & Cole, 1994, p. 81). Drug-related crimes, of course, were the particular target of mandatory sentencing, including even nonviolent drug crimes such as possession of marijuana (Cloud, 1999; Donziger, 1996, pp. 15, 25). The increase in the incarceration rate itself, and a corresponding increase in the lengths of sentences imposed, resulted in overcrowding and an increase in the costs of operating swelling prisons. As noted in Chapter 1, the vast majority of offenders caught up in this war were African American men. By the late 1980s prisons were extremely overcrowded and dangerous, with roughly two-thirds of U.S. correctional facilities under federal court orders to reduce overcrowding for violations of inmates' Eighth Amendment rights (Bohm & Haley, 1997, p. 327). As a result of the overcrowding crisis generated by mandatory sentencing schemes, jurisdictions looked to private vendors to fill the incarceration breach.

By 1999 there were thirteen private contractors operating adult correctional facilities in the United States, with a total bed space for 140,000 prisoners (Bureau of Justice Statistics, 1999, p. 82). The two largest of these—Corrections Corporation of America and Wackenhut Corrections Corporation—together held 80 percent of the total U.S. prisoners housed in private facilities. As documented in Table 6.1, it is also worth noting that CCA continues to dominate the prison privatization market, holding 52 percent of the available contracts, while Wackenhut holds roughly 22 percent (Abt Associates, Inc., 1998, p. 18). By comparison, then, Corrections Corporation of America's inmate population is larger than that of most state prison systems. In the late 1990s, for example, the state of Tennessee had an inmate population of roughly 17,000. Wackenhut's total inmate population for 1999 was 39,595 (Bureau of Justice Statistics, 1999, p. 82). In total, more than 150 private correctional facilities were operational in the United States in 1999 and housed roughly 5 percent of the total inmate population in the country (Abt Associates, Inc., 1998, app. 1, p. 2; Bureau of Justice Statistics, 1999, p. 82).

Ninety-five percent of inmates in private facilities have a minimum-security classification, with only 4 percent of privately held inmates having a maximum-security designation. At the end of 1997, only one private prison facility in operation was designated exclusively for maximum-security inmates—the South Bay Correctional Facility in Florida operated by Wackenhut (Abt Associates, Inc., 1998, p. 25). As the recently released Federal Bureau of Prisons study, *Private Prisons in the United States, 1999: An Assessment of Growth, Performance, Custody Standards, and*

Training Requirements concludes: "Compared to all prisoners held by state and federal prisons operated by public employees, the private sector has a disproportionate number of minimum security prisoners and few maximum security ones" (Camp & Gaes, 2000b, pp. 109–10). Targeting nonviolent minimum-security inmates, then, who typically require less discipline, need lower rates of medical care, and have less elaborate criminal histories, is the clear pattern of the industry (Camp & Gaes, 2002).

Crime Consciousness: Punishment as Socially Revealing

It is uncomfortable, certainly, to ponder the notion of *racist* law enforcement, as distinct from *neutral* or *fair* law enforcement. Although few would deny that race has played a central role in the creation of American social classes or the existing social order, people are still often very reluctant to extend their racial consciousness to law enforcement itself. Denying the fairness of law enforcement throws everything else out of whack: solving the crime problem might be more complex than simply hiring more police officers or building more prisons. As RAND Corporation (1997) has repeatedly found with its statistical analyses of mandatory sentencing, "getting tough" on crime without addressing the underlying causes of crime might ultimately be a waste of taxpayer money. Finally, if law—as it is actually enforced—disproportionately targets one group versus another, what socially harmful effects of law enforcement are being ignored? What social damage is unequal law enforcement itself causing?

The renewed appearance of private prisons, at this point in U.S. history, cannot be explained by charges of exploding crime rates (which are down dramatically over the past fifteen years), or the proven effectiveness of incarceration as a response to crime (long-term incarceration is both destructive to offenders and expensive to society), or the compelling cost-effectiveness of private-sector prisons (privatization of prisons does not save large amounts of money). Market-based business logic has not radically transformed the operation of prisons to make them more rehabilitative, socially just, or secure. Finally, as noted in Chapter 6, cost savings has not been the primary reason jurisdictions have adopted privatization in the first place: demand for bed space to house offenders caught up in the drug war has been the primary engine of for-profit imprisonment over the past twenty years.

In order to understand the reemergence of privatized prisons, one must dig deeper than the contemporary justifications put forward on their behalf (that private prisons save money, that private prisons are "better run" than state prisons, that market forces and "competition" order the social world in healthy ways). The profoundly high rate of imprisonment of young African American men from the inner city, the lack of regulatory oversight that characterizes the private prison industry despite an elaborate history of abuses, and the fact that the racial imbalances characterizing U.S. prisons today are hardly ever mentioned during legislative discussions of reinstituting private prisons all speak to race as the dominant but tellingly unspoken subtext of American criminal justice policy. As David Garland notes in his article "Punishment and Culture: The Symbolic Dimension of Criminal Justice":

> In truth, the established frameworks of cultural meaning undoubtedly influence the forms of punishment. But it is also the case that punishments and penal institutions help shape the overarching culture and contribute to the generation and regeneration of its terms. It is a two-way process—an interactive relationship—and if one is to think in terms of cause and effect or vectors of determination, then the arrows must run in both directions simultaneously (though they need not be of equal magnitude nor drawn on the same plane). . . . Penal institutions are thus "cause" as well as "effect," source as well as repository, of the cultural formations that give meaning to our social world. (1991, p. 193)

Dispossession and Incarceration: Poverty and Being Locked Up

As shown in the incarceration rate in Table 1.3, the disproportionate incarceration of African Americans also holds across genders, for both men and women. Programs seeking to remedy past racial discrimination, such as affirmative-action programs, however, have been very controversial. President Lyndon Johnson, purveyor of the War on Poverty and other programs such as affirmative action, once quipped that affirmative-action policies were the "right thing to do" but that they "would destroy the Democratic party" (Shorris, 1997, p. 208). After the Civil War, many white southerners became staunch Democrats in opposition to the party of Lincoln, the Republican Party. For many years right up until the 1960s, rural southern whites (and blacks, for that matter) who tended to be poor could be counted on to vote for Democratic candidates seeking to remedy their poverty. Democrat Robert F. Kennedy promised more aid to rural white southerners in West Virginia and throughout Appalachia in his own bid for the presidency in the 1960s.

As many scholars have pointed out, poverty has become an issue saturated with racial overtones about the deservedness of the poor for public help (Beckett, 1997). During the Great Depression Americans viewed poverty as a function of macrosocioeconomic collapse and were very willing to provide resources to those who needed assistance. Since that time, a moralistic shift in the public view of poverty has taken place, involving an explanation of poverty as a product of "laziness" or ineptitude of the impoverished. The dominant cultural explanation for poverty, in other words, has undergone a complete transformation since the time of the Great Depression—and now attributes individual moral failing as the cause of poverty rather than macroeconomic conditions affecting some neighborhoods and not others. Whereas past poverty and "public order" discussions focused on jobs, employment training, and worker placement, the new conservative paradigm focused on implementing wider use of punishment and reducing the size of government (Tonry & Petersilia, 2000; Wilson, 1996, 1999; Clear, 1997).

The larger mosaic of current political issues such as privatization, devolution, globalization, welfare reform, immigration policy, crime, and affirmative action all involve underlying debates about poverty, race, and governmental responsibility. Because a far greater proportion of African Americans and Hispanics live in poverty than whites, each of these issues is to a large extent racially contextualized (Garland, 2001a; Wilson, 1996; Parenti, 1999; C. West, 1999, p. 116). As Cornel West puts it:

> This age-old strategy of scapegoating the most vulnerable, frightening the most insecure and supporting the most comfortable constitutes a kind of iron law signaling the decline of modern civilizations, as in Tolstoy's Russia and Kafka's central Europe: chaotic and inchoate rebellion from below, withdrawal and retreat from public life from above and a desperate search for authoritarian law and order, at any cost, from the middle. (1999, p. 116)

Learning to Question Punishment

At the conclusion of this book, it is worth restating the central approach I have taken: a well-established tradition of viewing punishment—and imprisonment in particular—as serving agendas *other* than crime control has long existed in criminology. This tradition includes the work of

Emile Durkheim (1933), who argues that punishment enhances social solidarity; George Herbert Mead (1918), who contends that punishment releases inhibited social aggression; Georg Rusche and Otto Kirchheimer (1968), who maintain that incarceration rates fluctuate with labor and economic demand; Michel Foucault (1977), who views punishment strategies as part of a larger disciplinary strategy of social control; and David Garland (1990), who sees punishments as cultural expressions involving economic, moral, political, and functional aims.

The fact that our "crime wars" center almost exclusively on the behaviors of inner-city minorities also sends a socially revealing signal about our "crime consciousness." As critical legal studies scholars Austin Sarat and colleagues note: "What is true of law in general—its complexity, the interdependence among its constituent parts, its role in everyday life, and the status of folk knowledge as a form of legal action—is equally and especially true where the subject is crime and punishment" (Steiner, Bowers, & Sarat, 1999). Putting large numbers of black men once again into private prisons reveals something about today's prevailing social order: that race (still) plays a powerful role in the operation of the criminal justice system and its structuring of society.

This "culturalist" perspective on incarceration argues that systems of punishment always reflect and reinforce preexisting social and power relations (Garland, 1990). Pondered in this way, one comes to realize the truth of Durkheim's argument that certain segments of society both need and benefit from crime—and that criminality itself, in surprising ways, is an exploitable social resource for many in our society (see Beckett, 1997; and Chambliss, 2001).

The New Colonialism in Criminal Justice

There is no reason for you to try to become like white people and there is no basis whatever for their impertinent assumption that they must accept you. The really terrible thing, old buddy, is that you must accept them. And I mean that very seriously. You must accept them with love. For these innocent people have no other hope. They are, in effect, still trapped in a history which they do not understand; and until they understand it, they cannot be released from it. They had to believe for many years, and for innumerable reasons, that black men are inferior to white men. Many of them, indeed, know better, but, as you will discover, people find it very difficult to act on what they know.

—James Baldwin, "Letter to My Nephew," in *The Fire Next Time*

As in James Baldwin's passage above, Thomas Jefferson "knew better"—but found it "very difficult to act on" what he knew. According to criminologist Thorsten Sellin (1976), slavery and punishment have coexisted throughout history. That the Thirteenth Amendment simultaneously abolished slavery and initiated forced "involuntary servitude" for freed slaves in the United States speaks to this duality in the American context. Although the nature of prisoners' commodity value has changed somewhat in modern times—prisoners are no longer profitable solely for their labor, but almost exclusively now for their bodily ability to generate per diem payments to their private keepers—imprisonment for *private* profit is once again a viable economic industry in the United States (Hallett, 2002b).

As commitment to the welfare state's goals of social engineering becomes displaced by market-driven coping strategies designed to pacify increasingly vulnerable middle-class and even wealthy taxpayers, the focus of criminal justice policy and criminology itself has also changed (Johnson, 1988, p. 150; Melman, 2001; Frank, 2000). As for-profit mechanisms of social regulation expand globally, the populations on which this type of profit depends become more obviously disfranchised—"invisible"—embodying the kind of voicelessness characteristic of the dispossession of apartheid: in short, people who are politically nonthreatening, economically powerless, and socially reviled. In the United States and other Western countries, this dispossession affects people of color and "aliens" in far greater proportion than whites. The dispossessed have once again become the targets of private multinational corporate entrepreneurship: it was merchant shippers, after all, devising profitable schemes for the transport of human "cargo," who started the penal practice of transportation in the first place (Smith, 1965).

The most striking thing about the reemergence of capitalistic schemes with prisoners in America, however, is not that they have reappeared but that they should again involve the disproportionate captivity of African American men. According to the most recent data, 66 percent of inmates currently held in private prisons are racial minorities, with African Americans constituting the single largest group (43.9 percent black) (Austin & Coventry, 2001, p. 41). As Loic Wacquant points out, it is only since 1989 that African American men began again to dominate prison populations, as the drug war reached full implementation (1999, p. 215).

As best illustrated by the Thirteenth Amendment itself, for-profit prisons operate based on an understanding of prisoners as *private commodities*—an understanding that is unalterably tied in the United States to the tradition of indenture and slavery. As shown above, for-profit imprisonment first emerged with the operation of the Convict Lease system and dealt almost exclusively with people who had been African American slaves. The racial characteristics of modern private prisons, therefore, should not and cannot be ignored for what they still represent: a racialized for-profit imprisonment practice, still disproportionately utilizing young black men for its coercive system of economic production.

As Hal Pepinsky writes: "With my students, I come to a growing recognition that colonialism and capitalism are but the latest historical guise in which patriarchy becomes institutionalized" (2002, p. 3). As noted in Chapter 1, the pattern of disproportionate confinement primarily affects black men—but also Hispanic men. The same pattern exists with black women and Hispanic women, though on a far less grandiose scale. Today, minority males are those most profoundly victimized by mass imprisonment. Since the early 1960s, American criminal justice policy has undergone a profound transformation attributable to shifting sentiments about the welfare state and social welfare programs designed to help the poor that have resulted in more repressive strategies for controlling unemployment and individuals alleged to be threatening.

Privatized for-profit imprisonment schemes render the captive inmates a justifiable commodity, further weaken policy commitments to social programming for the poor, and maintain the lucrative persona of dark-skinned males as a "dangerous class" (Shelden, 2001).

Conclusion: Policy Recommendations

1. *Abandon the drug war.* The excessively high incarceration rates of the past twenty years have resulted in overcrowded and costly prisons, cultivating the classic high demand–low supply profit opportunities that have resurrected for-profit imprisonment. Strictly punitive responses to the problems of addiction have proven both ineffective and expensive time and again in American history. The U. .S Justice Department's own data reveal a profoundly high rate of recidivism, the highest of which is for drug crimes. Harsh mandatory sentencing schemes for most nonviolent crimes, especially as they have been shown to exacerbate the problems of the poor and disfranchised, should be eliminated as well. Even

socially conservative groups such as the American Bar Association have called for the abandonment of mandatory sentencing schemes (see the bar association's Kennedy Commission Report, cited below).

2. *Require strict monitoring and oversight of all existing private prison contracts.* Today in the United States, the for-profit imprisonment industry has become an unregulated behemoth, with serious problems in staff turnover, violence, and escapes. Although these problems are indeed also prevalent in public prisons, each time a private prison corporation is allowed to skirt the terms of a contract by, for example, not having as many guards as stipulated in the contract, the "hidden costs" of for-profit imprisonment increase. On a truly level playing field, where privatization "entrepreneurs" are forced to house a wide spectrum of inmates at all security levels (as in the public prison system), private industry will lose interest. Needless to say, no-bid contracts and statewide single-company contracts, as was attempted in Tennessee, must be forbidden outright, as they subvert the very "free-market" logic put forward by entrepreneurs on behalf of private prisons.

3. *Require basic criminal justice racial education.* In many American states, a foundational course required for high school graduation is U.S. government and American politics. Because criminal justice expenditures are today a central part of state and federal budgets—and because most Americans actually know very little about even basic issues in the field (such as our high recidivism and dramatically increasing incarceration rates)—*a required segment providing basic criminal justice education should be incorporated into all high school government classes.* As students review the framing of the Constitution and revisit the Civil War, connections should be made between the early rise of entrepreneurial imprisonment and its patently racialized context and the racial disproportions of today's prison population. Unfortunately, most Americans report that their dominant source of information about crime is the mass media, which distort the true nature of crime by fixating on violence and failing to report in accurate proportions the rate at which minorities are victimized and the high rate of "white" criminality (see Surette, 1998). The course could start by teaching critical thinking about crime, educating these future taxpayers about the extreme costs of incarceration relative to its benefits (a recidivism rate of near 70 percent), and covering basic information on victimization rates, recidivism, the dramatic rise in incarceration, and the racial proportions of our prison population. Reams of data showing that lower-class whites have higher crime rates

than middle-class blacks could be used to spark a serious reexamination of the underlying causes of crime and prompt a real discussion about racism in the criminal justice system and the merits of rehabilitation versus punishment.

4. *Share information and get active.* For-profit imprisonment has generated a lot of grassroots activism across the country, albeit rarely reported on in the mainstream press. Several state and national organizations exist that identify fighting proprietary prisons as a core issue. A few of the best of these are listed below. As mentioned in Chapter four, most instances of privatization have not been authorized by any public referendum, but have been instituted by executive order or subgovernmental fiat, as in the case of Tennessee. By and large, voters have not approved for-profit imprisonment as a policy option and have not been given the opportunity to reject it.

5. *Learn to question punishment.* Every single act of criminal punishment is an overtly *political* act. All such punishments utilize the authority of law and the power of the state in the name of "the people." When instances of mass imprisonment come to dominate the punishment process, deeper agendas beyond crime control must be posited and explored. As suggested throughout this book, broader agendas involving the profit motives of entrepreneurs, the aspirations of politicians, the tax-base desires of city planners, and a well-cultivated fear of crime in the body politic all combine to make the actual effectiveness of imprisonment for society an increasingly moot point. The social and fiscal costs associated with mass imprisonment must be brought to light and agendas for expansion of imprisonment scaled back.

6. *Abolish for-profit imprisonment* as the first step of a larger movement in decarceration of all nonviolent offenders in both public and private prisons.

Antiprivatization Activist Groups

American Bar Association
Justice Kennedy Commission on Mandatory Sentencing Report
http://www.abanet.org/family/council/6–22–04Sentencing.doc

Citizens against Private Prisons
http://capp.50megs.com

Families against Mandatory Minimums
http://www.famm.org/index2.htm

Grassroots Leadership
http://www.grassrootsleadership.org

Institute on Money in State Politics
http://www.followthemoney.org

November Coalition
http://www.november.org

Open Society Institute and Soros Foundations Network
http://www.soros.org/initiatives/issues/law

See also the Open Society Justice Initiative
http://www.justiceinitiative.org

NOTES

Chapter 1. Race, Crime, and For-Profit Imprisonment

1. By mid-2005, this was still the most reliable report on the racial makeup of private prison inmate populations.

2. As scholars of race are quick to point out, in the United States the designation "white" has less to do with skin color than social status. Italian and Irish immigrants, for example, only slowly came to be considered "white" (Lopez, 1995).

3. In an interesting aside, Kimberle Crenshaw makes note of bell hooks's open criticism of Cornel West's use of "language that was inaccessible and mystifying" to people who were disfranchised or excluded from the academy (2002, p. 1359n17). In another interesting note, Crenshaw mulls over this question: "Was CRT a product of people of color, or was CRT a product of any scholar engaged in a critical reflection of race?" (p. 1363). After stating that she subscribes to the latter proposition, she adds in a footnote about the "traditional exclusion of whites" from some CRT workshops: "The issue is somewhat academic at this point in light of a growing body of critical articles on race written by white colleagues. Alan Freeman, Gary Peller, Barbara Flagg, and Duncan Kennedy are just a few Anglo scholars whose articles are key texts within CRT" (p. 1363n22).

4. As the Federal Bureau of Prisons study titled *Private Prisons in the United States, 1999: An Assessment of Growth, Performance, Custody Standards, and Training Requirements* states: "Compared to all prisoners held by state and federal prisons operated by public employees, the private sector has a disproportionate number of minimum security prisoners and few maximum security ones" (Camp & Gaes 2000b, pp. 109–10).

Chapter 2. For-Profit Imprisonment in American History

1. By 1897, however, a year after the ominous *Plessy v. Fergusson* case legalizing racial segregation, David Potter notes: "Finally, in 1897 the Louisiana Bourbon Democrats sought to deal once and for all with the problem of dissent by eliminating from the voting rolls as many potential dissenters as possible. The new state constitution of that year, by means of literacy and property qualifications, either discouraged or directly prevented the subsequent registration of nearly all Negro voters. . . . Black voter registration in Louisiana declined from 130,344 in 1897 to 5,320 in 1900" (1972, p. 33n5).

2. Curtin documents the existence of a small number of female convict laborers (2000, pp. 113–29). Although most of the female prisoners under the Convict Lease system were black, the solid majority of white women incarcerated under it were there for "felonious adultery," "a crime which implied interracial sex" (p. 114).

3. A recent contemporary example of this comes from the state of Florida's Department of Corrections, which recently fined the Aramark Corporation—a privately owned and operated food service company providing food for Florida's prison inmates—$110,000 for failing to provide inmates with enough food ("Prisons Need"). Related charges of watering down food, reusing uneaten portions of beef, and running "filthy" kitchens were documented by corrections officers.

4. Thomas Jefferson's first draft of the Declaration of Independence "charged that the king was personally to blame for the slave trade" and had explicit language abolishing slavery as a scourge on the doctrine of freedom. According to Jefferson, the language written into the Declaration of Independence "reprobating enslaving the inhabitants of Africa was struck out in complaisance to South Carolina and Georgia, who had never attempted to restrain the importation of slaves and who, on the contrary still wished to continue it. Our northern brethren also, I believe, felt a little tender under those censures, for, though their people have very few slaves themselves, yet they had been pretty considerable carriers of them to others" (quoted in Randall, 1993, p. 275).

Chapter 3. Capitalist Crime Control

1. As widely noted in the research on private prisons, one of the key strategies private prison companies use in cost cutting is keeping wages and especially benefits of employees low (Austin & Coventry, 2001).

Chapter 4. Money and Power

1. I have already discussed why, in regards to the private prison industry in the United States, the "military industrial complex" metaphor remains unpersuasive—primarily due to the plethora of local players with no direct stake in sentencing outcomes involved in generating prisoners and, in the case of private prisons, the macrolevel and historical social forces embedded in the operation of for-profit imprisonment.

2. The Tennessee Select Oversight Committee on Corrections study, titled *Comparative Evaluation of Privately Managed Corrections Corporation of America Prison (South Central Correctional Center) and State-Managed Prototypical Prisons (Northeast Correctional Center, Northwest Correctional Center)* (1995), was conducted in two phases, one assessing operational costs and the other assessing quality of service. The study compared three multicustody (minimum to maximum inmate classification) prisons for male inmates. Findings from the study include the following: "Using data that covered July 1993 through July 1994, the study concluded that the costs of operating the private and both state facilities were virtually identical" (as cited in U.S. General Accounting Office, 1996, p. 25). The SOCC study also noted: "The cost after adjustment for the allocation to the three facilities shows an average cost for the state facilities of $35.23 per day versus $35.39 for the CCA facility, or a difference of less that one half of 1%" (1995, p. 2). The U.S. General Accounting Office further stated: "The overall performance scores were 98.49 for the private facility and 97.17 and 98.34, respectively, for the two public facilities" (1996, p. 25).

3. This violates a fundamental guideline for privatization offered by the U.S. Department of Justice: that independent monitors be part of the legislatively authorized use of privatization (see National Institute of Justice, 1987).

4. The subtitle to this section is a phrase I borrowed from Randall Shelden.

Chapter 5. Bad Faith

1. Zald goes on to note that, despite this emphasis on symbolism, Gusfield himself "quotes Jellineck to the effect that during Prohibition alcohol consumption was cut in half." Zald, therefore, concludes that even by Gusfield's account, "Prohibition was not all purely symbolic" in its agenda, but instrumental as well (1964, p. 392).

2. DiIulio has since recanted his support for mandatory minimums and "regrets" using the term *superpredator*, saying to the *Washington Post:* "I went too far. I regret describing [juvenile offenders] in such a dehumanizing way" (Morin, 2001). Attributing his change in heart to his recent conversion to Catholicism, DiIulio also stated recently in an interview with the *New York Times:* "Prevention is the only reasonable way to approach these problems" (Becker, 2001).

Chapter 6. The Easy Inmate Market

1. The National Institute of Justice asks, "What evaluation criteria should be used?" in reference to request-for-proposal responses from private contractors. As top priorities, the institute lists: "quality, relevancy, or recency of projects of a similar nature conducted or completed by the contractor and ability to meet time constraints" (1987, p. 33).

2. Wackenhut recently became part of Group 4 Securicor, "the world's largest provider of security services" (http://www.wackenhut.com).

REFERENCES

Abt Associates, Inc. (1998). *Private prisons in the United States: An assessment of current practice.* Cambridge, Mass.: Abt Associates.

Africa News Service. (2002, February 1). New prison to alleviate overcrowding.

Aldrich, M. (1998, September 19). Firm's imported inmates endanger Tenn, lawmaker says. *Memphis Commercial Appeal*, p. A11.

Associated Press. (1997, August 18). State says CCA rates too high. *Nashville Tennessean*, p. B1.

———. (1998a, March 11). Panel gives opinion of privatized prisons in Tennessee. *Memphis Commercial Appeal*, p. A12.

———. (1998b, April 8). Privatization issue losing momentum. *Memphis Commercial Appeal*, p. B2.

Austin, J., & G. Coventry. (2001). *Emerging issues on privatized prisons.* Washington, D.C.. National Council on Crime and Delinquency.

———. (2003). A second look at the private prison debate. *Criminologist, 28*(5), 1–3, 5.

Austin, J., & J. Irwin. (2001). *It's about time: America's imprisonment binge* (3rd ed.). Boston: Wadsworth Publishing.

Ayers, E. L. (1984). *Vengeance and justice: Crime and punishment in the 19th century American South.* New York: Oxford University Press.

Baldwin, J. (1963). *The fire next time.* New York: Dial Press.

Bales, W. D., L. B. Bedard, S. T. Quinn, D. T. Ensley, & G. P. Holley. (2005). Recidivism of public and private state prison inmates in Florida. *Criminology & Public Policy, 4*(1), 57–82.

Balkin, J. M. (1991). Review essay: Ideology as constraint. *Stanford Law Review, 43,* 1133–69.

Bates, E. (1998, January 5). Prisons for profit. *Nation, 5,* 11–26.

Baumer, E. (1994). Poverty, crack, and crime: A cross-city analysis. *Journal of Research in Crime and Delinquency, 31,* 311–27.

Beaumont, G. de, & A. de Tocqueville. (1964). *On the penitentiary system in the United States and its application in France.* Carbondale: Southern Illinois University Press.

Becker, E. (2001, February 9). As ex-theorist on young "superpredators," Bush aide has regrets. *New York Times,* p. A19.

Becker, H. (1963). *Outsiders: Studies in the sociology of deviance.* London: Free Press.

Beckett, K. (1997). *Making crime pay.* New York: Oxford University Press.

Beckett, K., & T. Sasson. (2000a). *The politics of injustice.* Thousand Oaks, Calif.: Sage.

———. (2000b). The war on crime as hegemonic strategy: A neo-Marxian theory of the new punitiveness in U.S. criminal justice policy. In S. S. Simpson (Ed.), *Of crime & criminality: The use of theory in everyday life* (pp. 61–84). Boston: Pine Forge Press.

Benson, B. L. (1998). *To serve and protect: Privatization and community in criminal justice.* Oakland, Calif.: Independent Institute.

Bernard, T. J. (1983). *The consensus-conflict debate: Form and content in social theories.* New York: Columbia University Press.

Bierne, P., & J. Messerschmidt. (2000). *Criminology* (3rd ed.). Boulder: Westview Press.

Blankenship, S., & E. Yanarella. (2001). Prisons as a policy tool of local economic development: Outcomes and Impact. Paper presented at the 2001 annual meeting of the Academy of Criminal Justice Sciences, Washington, D.C.

Bohm, R. M., & K. Haley. (1997). *Introduction to criminal justice.* New York: Glencoe/McGraw Hill.

Bonczar, T., & A. J. Beck. (1997). *Lifetime likelihood of going to state or federal prison.* Washington, D.C.: U.S. Department of Justice.

Borna, S. (1986). Free enterprise goes to prison. *British Journal of Criminology, 26*(4), 321–34.

Bosworth, M., & E. Carrabine. (2001). Reassessing resistance: Race, gender, and sexuality in prison. *Punishment & Society, 3*(4), 501–15.

Bowditch, C., & R. Everett. (1991). Private prisons are not more efficient than public prisons. In R. Espejo (Ed.), *America's prisons: Opposing viewpoints* (pp. 27–30). San Diego: Greenhaven Press.

Bozovic, M. (Trans.). (1995). *The panopticon writings,* by Jeremy Bentham. New York: Verso.

Buechner, T. S. (1972). *Norman Rockwell: A sixty year retrospective.* New York: Harry Abrams Publishers.

Bureau of Justice Statistics. (1995). *Sourcebook on criminal justice statistics.* Albany, NY: U.S. Department of Justice.

———. (1996). *Correctional populations in the United States, 1994.* Washington, D.C.: U.S. Department of Justice.

———. (1999). *Sourcebook of criminal justice statistics, 1999.* Washington, D.C.: U.S. Department of Justice.

Burns, W. H. (1998). Law and race in early America. In D. Kairys (Ed.), *The politics of law: A progressive critique* (pp. 1–20). Boston: Basic Books.

Bursick, R., & H. Grasmick. (1993). Economic deprivation and neighborhood crime rates, 1960–1980. *Law & Society Review, 27,* 263–78.

Butterfield, F. (2002, June 3). Study shows building prisons did not prevent repeat crimes. *New York Times,* p. A11.

Byrne, J., & R. Sampson. (Eds.). (1986). *The social ecology of crime.* New York: Springer Verlag.

Camp, S. D., & G. G. Gaes. (2000a). Private adult prisons: What do we really know and why don't we know more? In D. Shichor & M. Gilbert (Eds.), *Privatization in criminal justice: Past, present, & future* (pp. 283–98). Cincinnati: Anderson Publishing.

———. (2000b). *Private prisons in the United States, 1999: An assessment of growth, performance, custody standards, and training requirements.* Washington, D.C.: U.S. Federal Bureau of Prisons.

———. (2002). Growth and quality of U.S. private prisons: Evidence from a national survey. *Criminology & Public Policy, 1*(3), 427–50.

Carleton, M. T. (1971). *Politics and punishment: The history of the Louisiana state penal system.* Baton Rouge: Louisiana State University Press.

Carr, R. (2001, April 8). DiIulio driven by values of his boyhood. *Atlanta Journal Constitution,* p. 5F.

CCA deal breakdown: Drops shares 22%. (1997, March 21). *Nashville Banner,* p. D2.

CCA loses Supreme Court "test" case. (1997, June 24). *Nashville Tennessean,* p. B1.

Chambliss, W. J. (2001). *Power, politics, & crime.* Boulder: Westview Press.

Chambliss, W. J., & D. Seidman. (1971). *Law, order, & power.* Reading, Mass.: Addison-Wesley.

Chaptman, D. (2002). Jobs saved in legislator's area. *Milwaukee Journal Sentinel.* http://www.jsonline.com/news/state/jul02/57837.asp.

Chesteen, R. D. (1998). The Tennessee prison system: A study of evolving public policy in state corrections. In J. Vile & M. Byrnes (Eds.), *Tennessee government and politics: Democracy in the Volunteer State* (pp. 167–81). Westport, Conn.: Greenwood Press.

Christianson, S. (1998). *With liberty for some: 500 years of imprisonment in America*. Boston: Northeastern University Press.

Christie, N. (1993). *Crime control as industry: Gulags Western style*. New York: Routledge.

Clear, T. (1997). Societal responses to the president's crime commission: A thirty-year retrospective. In *The challenge of crime in a free society: Looking back, looking forward* (pp. 131–58). Washington, D.C.: National Institute of Justice.

Clear, T., & G. F. Cole. (1994). *American corrections*. Boston: Wadsworth.

Cloud, J. (1999, February 1). A get-tough policy that failed. *Time, 153*(4), 48–51.

Cobb, R., & C. D. Elder. (1972). *Participation in American politics: The dynamics of agenda-building*. Boston: Allyn and Bacon.

Cobb, R., J. Keith-Ross, & M. H. Ross. (1976). Agenda building as a comparative political process. *American Political Science Review, 70*, 126–38.

Cohn, J. (1989). *Creating America: George Horace Lorimer and the Saturday Evening Post*. Pittsburgh: University of Pittsburgh Press.

Cole, G. F. (1994). *The American system of criminal justice* (6th ed.). Boston: Wadsworth.

Coles, R. (1978). *Children of crisis*. Boston: Little, Brown.

———. (2000). "Ruby bridges and a painting." In M. Hennessey & A. Knutson, *Norman Rockwell: Pictures for the American people* (pp. 105–14). New York: Harry Abrams Publishers.

Colvin, M. (1997). *Penitentiaries, reformatories, and chain gangs: Social theory and the history of punishment in nineteenth-century America*. New York: St. Martin's Press.

Cooper, R. (2001, February 18). For new post, Bush puts faith in an unlikely champion of the needy. *Los Angeles Times*, p. A15.

Corrections Corp. cuts costs, doubles income. (1997, June 1). *Nashville Banner*, p. D2.

Corrections Corporation of America. (1985, fall). *Private Line* (3). Newsletter.

———. (2003). CCA working with Institute in Basic Life Principles to create faith-based program: New program to encourage rehabilitation. Press release. http://biz.yahoo.com/bw/040315/155209_1.html.

Cottrol, R. J., & R. T. Diamond. (1995). The Second Amendment: Toward an Afro-Americanist reconsideration. In R. Delgado (Ed.), *Critical race theory: The cutting edge* (pp. 15–23). Philadelphia: Temple University Press.

Court rejects immunity for CCA prison guards: Ruling may slow push to privatization. (1997, June 23). *Nashville Banner*, p. A4.

Crenshaw, K. W. (2002). Critical race studies: The first decade: Critical reflections; or, A foot in the closing door." *UCLA Law Review, 49*, 1343–72.

Currie, E. (1993). *Reckoning: Drugs, the cities, and the American future*. New York: Hill & Wang.

———. (1998). *Crime and punishment in America*. New York: Metropolitan Books.

Curtin, M. E. (2000). *Black prisoners and their world, Alabama, 1865–1900.* Charlottesville: University Press of Virginia.

Daly, K., & L. Maher. (1998). *Criminology at the crossroads: Feminist readings in crime and justice.* New York: Oxford University Press.

Davis, A. (1998). Reflections on the prison industrial complex. *ColorLines,* 1(2), 1–8. Also available online at http://www.arc.org/C_Lines/CLArchive/story1_2_01.html.

DeKeseredy, W., & M. Schwartz. (1996). *Contemporary criminology.* Boston: Wadsworth.

Delgado, R. (1995). Critique of liberalism. In R. Delgado (Ed.), *Critical race theory: The cutting edge* (p. 1). Philadelphia: Temple University Press.

DiIulio, J. (1993). The duty to govern: A critical perspective on the private management of prisons and jails. In R. C. Monk (Ed.), *Taking sides: Clashing views on controversial issues in crime and criminology* (pp. 135–45). Columbus, Ohio: McGraw-Hill/Dushkin.

Donziger, S. R. (Ed.). (1996). *The real war on crime: The report of the National Criminal Justice Commission.* New York: Harper Collins.

DuBois, W. E. B. (2002 [1901]). The spawn of slavery. In S. Gabbidon, E. Greene, & V. Young (Eds.), *African American classics in criminology & criminal justice* (pp. 83–88). Thousand Oaks, Calif.: Sage.

Duffee, D. E., & E. F. McGarrell. (1990). *Community corrections: A community field approach.* Cincinnati: Anderson Publishing.

Durkheim, E. (1933). *The division of labor in society.* New York: Free Press.

Dyer, J. (2000). *The perpetual prisoner machine.* Boulder: Westview Press.

Egelko, B. (2004, March 8). Verdict on "3 strikes" law mixed after first 10 years. *Washington Post,* p. B1.

Elias, N. (1978 [1939]). *The civilizing process.* Vol. 1, *The history of manners.* Oxford: Blackwell.

———. (1982 [1939]). *The civilizing process.* Vol. 2, *State formation and civilization.* Oxford: Blackwell.

Elliot, A. R. (2002, December 31). Locking up more business, a cell at a time. *Investor's Business Daily.* http://www.investors.com.

Elsner, A. (2001, December 3). U.S. Immigration holds thousands of youths in jail. *Reuters News Service.*

Engle, D. (1996). Law in the domains of everyday life: The construction of community and difference. In A. Sarat & T. Kearns (Eds.), *Law in everyday life* (pp. 123–90). Ann Arbor: University of Michigan Press.

Epstein, E. (1977). *Agency of fear: Opiates and political power in America.* New York: Putnam.

Ericson, R., M. McMahon, & D. G. Evans. (1993). Punishing for profit: Reflections on the revival of privatization in corrections. *Canadian Journal of Criminology,* 29(4), 355–87.

Ethridge, P., & J. Marquart. (1993). Private prisons in Texas: The new penology for profit. *Justice Quarterly,* 10(1), 29–48.

Evans, D. T., F. Cullen, & G. R. Dunaway. (1995). Religion and crime reexamined: The impact of religion, secular controls, and social ecology on adult criminality. *Criminology, 33*(3), 195–224.

Feeley, M. M. (2002). Entrepreneurs of punishment: The legacy of privatization. *Punishment & Society, 4*(3), 321–44.

Felson, M. (1994). *Crime and everyday life.* Thousand Oaks, Calif.: Pine Forge Press.

Ferrar, R. (1997, June 8). Prison privatization bill leads list of bills that failed to pass. *Knoxville News-Sentinel,* p. A4.

Fierce, M. C. (1994). *Slavery revisited: Blacks and the southern convict lease system, 1865–1933.* New York: City University of New York Press.

Finch, C. (1975). *Norman Rockwell's America.* New York: Harry Abrams Publishers.

Fitzgerald, R. (1991). Private prisons: More effective than public prisons? In R. Espejo (Ed.), *America's prisons: Opposing viewpoints* (pp. 114–15). San Diego: Greenhaven Press.

Ford, R. (2002, May 15). Tens of thousands to be held in for-profit rural detention centres. *London Times.*

Foucault, M. (1977). *Discipline and punish: The birth of the prison.* London: Pantheon.

Frank, T. (2000). *One market under God: Extreme capitalism, market populism, and the end of economic democracy.* New York: Doubleday.

Fraser, R. (2001, November 1). Captive workers, captive market. *Washington Post,* p. A35.

Freeman, R. B. (2001). Does the booming economy help explain the fall in crime? In *Perspectives on crime and justice: 1999–2000 lecture series* (pp. 23–50). Washington, D.C.: U.S. Department of Justice.

Friedman, L. (1999). On stage: Some historical notes about criminal justice. In P. Ewick, R. Kagan, & A. Sarat (Eds.), *Social science, social policy, and the law* (pp. 68–100). New York: Russell Sage Foundation.

Furman v. Georgia, 408 U.S. 238 (1972).

Garland, D. (1990). *Punishment and modern society: A study in social theory.* Chicago: University of Chicago Press.

———. (1991). Punishment and culture: The symbolic dimension of criminal justice. *Studies in Law, Politics, & Society, 11,* 191–224.

———. (1996). The limits of the sovereign state. *British Journal of Criminology, 36*(4), 445–71.

———. (2001a). *The culture of control: Crime and social order in contemporary society.* Chicago: University of Chicago Press.

———. (2001b). Introduction: The meaning of mass imprisonment. In D. Garland (Ed.), *Mass imprisonment: Social causes and consequences* (pp. 1–3). Thousand Oaks, Calif.: Sage.

Garland, D., & R. Sparks. (2000). *Criminology and social theory.* New York: Oxford University Press.

Gilbert, M. J. (2000a). How much is too much privatization in criminal justice? In D. Shichor & M. Gilbert (Eds.), *Privatization in criminal justice: Past, present, & future* (pp. 41–78). Cincinnati: Anderson Publishing.

———. (2000b). Not a true partner: Local politics and jail privatization in Frio County. In D. Shichor & M. Gilbert (Eds.), *Privatization in criminal justice: Past, present, & future* (pp. 171–206). Cincinnati: Anderson Publishing.

Gilligan, J. (1996). *Violence: Reflections on a national epidemic.* New York: Vintage Books.

Goffman, E. (1961). *Asylums: Essays on the social situation of mental patients and other inmates.* Cambridge, Mass.: Blackwell.

Gold, S. D. (1995). *The fiscal crisis of the states: Lessons for the future.* Washington, D.C.: Georgetown University Press.

Goldstein, P. J., H. Brownstein, P. J. Ryan, & P. Bellucci. (1997). Crack and homicide in New York City: A case study in the epidemiology of violence. In C. Reinarman and H. G. Levine (Eds.), *Crack in America: Demon drugs and social justice* (pp. 113–30). Berkeley and Los Angeles: University of California Press.

Greenberg, D. F., & V. West. (2001). State prison populations and their growth, 1971–1991. *Criminology, 39*(3), 615–53.

Gregory, D. L. (1987). Review of *A guide to critical legal studies,* by M. Kelman. *Duke Law Journal,* 1138.

Gusfield, J. (1963). *Symbolic crusade: Status politics and the American temperance movement.* Urbana: University of Illinois Press.

Hagan, J. (1989). *Structural criminology.* New Brunswick, N.J.: Rutgers University Press.

———. (1994). *Crime and disrepute.* Thousand Oaks, Calif.: Pine Forge Press.

Hallett, M. A. (1996). The social dimensions of prison labor laws: The Hawes-Cooper Act. In M. McShane & F. Williams (Eds.), *Encyclopedia of American Prisons* (pp. 230–32). New York: Garland Publishing.

———. (1997). Statement on the proposed privatization of Tennessee's prison system. Paper delivered to Tennessee Corrections Oversight Committee, Nashville, Tenn., May 15.

———. (2001). An introduction to prison privatization: Issues for the 21st century. In R. Muraskin & A. Roberts (Eds.), *Visions for change: Criminal justice in the 21st century* (pp. 371–389). New York: Prentice-Hall.

———. (2002a). Faith-based corrections as symbolic crusade. *Humanity & Society, 25*(4), 219–38.

———. (2002b). Race, crime, and for-profit imprisonment: Social disorganization as market opportunity. *Punishment & Society: The International Journal of Penology, 4*(3), 369–93.

Hallett, M. A., & A. Hanauer. (2001). Selective celling: Inmate population in Ohio's private prisons. Cleveland: Policy Matters Ohio.

Hallett, M. A., & J. F. Lee. (2000). Public money, private interests: The grass roots battle against CCA in Tennessee. In D. Shichor & M. Gilbert (Eds.),

Privatization in criminal justice: Past, present, & future (pp. 227–44). Cincinnati: Anderson Publishing.

Hallinan, J. T. (2001). *Going up the river: Travels in a prison nation.* New York: Random House.

————. (2002, May 1). Charity lends a hand to prisons with murky off-the-books deals. *Wall Street Journal,* p. A1.

Harden, C. (2002, July 23). Private prisons fill void left by plant closings. *Jackson (Miss.) Clarion-Ledger,* http://www.clarionledger.com/news/0206/23/m01b.html.

Harding, R. W. (1997). *Private prisons and public accountability.* New Brunswick, N.J.: Transaction Publishers.

Harrell, A., O. Mitchell, A. Hirst, D. Marlowe, & J. Merrill. (2002). Breaking the cycle of drugs and crime: Findings from the Birmingham BTC demonstration. *Criminology & Public Policy, 1*(2), 189–216.

Harrison, P., & A. Beck. (2004). *Prisoners in 2003.* Washington, D.C.: Bureau of Justice Statistics.

Hartmann, S. (1998, August 2). A private solution: Governments put corrections in companies' hands despite problems. *Nashville Tennessean,* p. E1.

Henry, S., & D. Milovanovic. (1999). Introduction: Postmodernism and constitutive theory. In S. Henry & D. Milovanovic (Eds.), *Constitutive criminology at work: Applications to crime and justice* (pp. 3–16). Albany: SUNY Press.

Hill-Collins, P. (1991). *Black feminist thought: Knowledge, consciousness, and the politics of empowerment.* New York: Routledge.

hooks, bell. (1992). *Black looks: Race and representation.* Boston: South End Press.

————. (2000). *All about love: New visions.* New York: Perennial.

Hughes, R. (1987). *The fatal shore.* New York: Random House.

Humphrey, T. (1997, April 18). Labor, state employees at odds over prison privatization plan. *Knoxville News-Sentinel,* p. A1.

————. (1998, May 24). Legislature listens where money talks: Lobbyists' track records tied to fatness of purses. *Knoxville News-Sentinel,* p. A1.

Inglis Thomson, C. (1997). Black and white. Review of *Critical race theory: The cutting edge* and *Critical race theory: The key writings that formed the movement. California Law Review, 85,* 1647–86.

Irwin, J., & J. Austin. (1996). *It's about time: America's imprisonment binge.* Boston: Wadsworth Publishing.

Jackson, J. (2003, March 11). Editorial on mandatory sentencing. *Chicago Sun-Times.*

Jacoby, J. (2001, November 11). Monopolists behind bars. *Boston Globe,* p. E7.

James, S. (2002, May 2). Private prison operators upbeat on results. *Reuters News Service.*

————. (2003, March 3). Budget crunch may help private prisons. *Reuters News Service.*

Johnson, B. R., S. J. Jang, D. B. Larson, & S. De Li. (2000a). Does adolescent religious commitment matter? A reexamination of the effects of religiosity in delinquency. *Journal of Research in Crime and Delinquency, 38*(1), 22–44.

Johnson, B., D. B. Larson, S. De Li, & S. J. Jang. (2000b). Escaping from the crime of inner cities: Church attendance and religious salience among disadvantaged youth. *Justice Quarterly, 17*(2), 377–91.

Johnson, H. (1988). *History of criminal justice.* Cincinnati: Anderson Publishing.

Justice Policy Institute. (2002). *Cellblocks or classrooms? The funding of higher education and corrections and its impact on African American men.* Washington, D.C.: Justice Policy Institute.

Kairys, D. (Ed.). (1998). *The politics of law. A progressive critique.* New York: Basic Books.

Kennedy, D. (1998). Legal education as training for hierarchy. In D. Kairys (Ed.), *The politics of law: A progressive critique* (pp. 54–78). New York: Basic Books.

Kennedy, R. (1997). *Race, crime, and the law.* New York: Vintage Books.

Kyle, J. (1998). The privatization debate continues: Tennessee's experience highlights scope of controversy over private prisons. *Corrections Today, 60*(5), 88.

Lang, K. (1964). Review of *Symbolic crusade: Politics and the American temperance movement,* by J. Gusfield. *American Sociological Review, 29*(5), 768–69.

Langan, P. A., & D. J. Levin. (2002). *Recidivism of prisoners released in 1994.* Washington, D.C.: U.S. Department of Justice.

Larkin, S. (2002, January 19). Woomera detainees sew lips together. *Daily Telegraph,* p. 2.

Lauritsen, J., & R. Sampson. (1998). Minorities, crime, and criminal justice. In M. Tonry (Ed.), *The handbook of crime and punishment* (pp. 58–84). New York: Oxford University Press.

Lewis, O. F. (1967 [1922]). *The development of American prisons and prison customs, 1776–1845.* Montclair, N.J.: Patterson Smith Publishing.

Lichtenstein, A. (1996). *Twice the work of free labor: The political economy of convict labor in the New South.* New York: Verso.

———. (2001). The private and the public in penal history. In D. Garland (Ed.), *Mass imprisonment: Social causes and consequences* (pp. 171–78). Thousand Oaks, Calif.: Sage.

Liebling, A. (2004). *Prisons and their moral performance: A study of values, quality, and prison life.* New York: Oxford University Press.

Lilly, J. R., & P. Knepper. (1993). The corrections-commercial complex. *Crime & Delinquency, 39*(2), 150–66.

Locker, R. (1997a, April 23). Firm hoping to run private prisons writing bill creating them. *Memphis Commercial Appeal,* p. A1.

———. (1997b, May 23). Prison bill won't see action by end of this session: Privatization foes cheer decision. *Memphis Commercial Appeal,* p. B1.

———. (1997c, May 25). Personal, political, business ties bind CCA, state. *Memphis Commercial Appeal*, p. B3.

———. (1998, April 15). Vote-starved prison bill dies: Workers cheer but Tenn privatization may revive in '99. *Memphis Commercial Appeal*, p. A1.

Logan, C. (1990). *Private prisons: Cons and pros.* New York: Oxford University Press.

Logan, C., & B. W. McGriff. (1989). *Comparing costs of public and private prisons.* Washington, D.C.: National Institute of Justice.

Lopez, I. H. (1995). The social construction of race. In R. Delgado (Ed.), *Critical race theory: The cutting edge* (pp. 191–203). Philadelphia: Temple University Press.

Lynch, M. J., & E. B. Patterson. (1990). Racial discrimination in the criminal justice system: Evidence from four jurisdictions. In B. MacLean & D. Milovanovic (Eds.), *Racism, empiricism, and criminal justice* (pp. 51–60). Vancouver, B.C.: Collective Press.

Maguire, K., & A. Pastore. (Eds.). (2002). *Sourcebook of criminal justice statistics.* Washington, D.C.: U.S. Department of Justice.

Mancini, M. J. (1978). Race, economics, and the abandonment of convict leasing. *Journal of Negro History, 63*(4), 339–352.

———. (1996). *One dies, get another: Convict leasing in the American South, 1866–1928.* Columbia: University of South Carolina Press.

Mann, C. R., & M. Zatz. (Eds.). (1998). *Images of color, images of crime: Readings.* Los Angeles: Roxbury Publishing.

Marcott, A. (2002, July 17). Prison employees in limbo after delay sets opening back until 2003. *Marshfield (Wisc.) News-Herald.* Available online at http://www.wisinfo.com/newsherald/mnhlocal/276165623193174.shtml.

Mauer, M. (2000). Young black Americans and the criminal justice system. In J. James (Ed.), *States of confinement: Policing, detention, and prisons* (pp. 75–84). New York: St. Martin's Press.

McCarthy, B. R. (1987). *Intermediate punishments: Intensive supervision, home confinement, and electronic surveillance.* New York: Willow Tree Press.

McCarty, P. (2002, June 21). Corrections industry: Safe place to lock away investments. *Dow Jones Newswires.* http://www.dowjones.com.

McGarrell, E. F., & T. Castellano. (1991). An integrative conflict model of the criminal law formation process. *Journal of Research in Crime and Delinquency, 28,* 174–96.

McKelvey, B. (1977). *American prisons: A history of good intentions.* Montclair, N.J.: Patterson Smith Publishing.

Mead, G. H. (1918). The psychology of punitive justice. *American Journal of Sociology, 23,* 577–602.

Melman, S. (2001). *After capitalism: From managerialism to workplace democracy.* New York: Alfred A. Knopf.

Mench, E. (1998). The history of mainstream legal thought. In D. Kairys (Ed.), *The politics of law: A progressive critique* (pp. 25–53). Boston: Basic Books.

Messerschmidt, J. (1986). *Capitalism, patriarchy, and crime: Toward a socialist feminist criminology*. Totowa, N.J.: Rowman and Littlefield.

Miller, J. (1996). *Search and destroy: African-American males in the criminal justice system*. Cambridge: Cambridge University Press.

Morin, R. (2001, February 26). Leading with his right: John DiIulio, ready to go to the mat with a faith-based approach to crime. *Washington Post*, p. C1.

Morris, N., & D. J. Rothman. (1995). *Oxford history of the prison: The practice of punishment in Western society*. New York: Oxford University Press.

Morrison, T. (1997). Home. In W. Lubiano (Ed.), *The house that race built: Black Americans, U.S. terrain* (pp. 3–12). New York: Pantheon Books.

National Institute of Justice. (1987). *Issues in contracting for the private operation of prisons and jails*. Washington, D.C.: U.S. Department of Justice.

Oberweis, T., & M. Musheno. (2001). *Knowing rights: State actors' stories of power, identity, and morality*. Burlington, Vt.: Ashgate/Dartmouth.

Olasky, M. (1992). *The tragedy of American compassion*. Washington, D.C.: Regnery Gateway Publishing.

———. (2000). *Compassionate conservatism: What it is, what it does, and how it can transform America*. New York: Free Press.

Olivas, M. A. (1995). The chronicles, my grandfather's stories, and immigration law: The slave traders chronicle as racial history. In R. Delgado (Ed.), *Critical race theory: The cutting edge* (pp. 9–20). Philadelphia: Temple University Press.

Oshinsky, D. M. (1996). *Worse than slavery: Parchman Farm and the ordeal of Jim Crow justice*. New York: Free Press.

Palumbo, D. (1986). Privatization and corrections policy. *Policy Studies Review*, 5, 598–605.

———. (1994). *Public policy in America: Government in action*. New York: Harcourt Brace.

Parenti, C. (1999). *Lockdown America: Police and prisons in the age of crisis*. New York: Verso.

Pepinsky, H. (2002). Toward the decolonization of responses to violence. Address to the Tenth International Conference on Penal Abolition (ICOPA X). Abuja, Nigeria, August 22.

Pepinsky, H. E., & R. Quinney. (1991). *Criminology as peacemaking*. Bloomington: Indiana University Press.

Petersilia, J. (1994). Debating crime and imprisonment in California. *Evaluation & Program Planning*, 17(2), 165–77.

Platt, A. (1977). *The child savers: The invention of delinquency*. Chicago: University of Chicago Press.

Potter, D. M. (1972). *The colonial idiom*. Carbondale: Southern Illinois University Press.

Prisons need better food service. (2002, July 2). *St. Petersburg Times*, editorial page.

Push for privatization boosts CCA. (1997, May 9). *Nashville Tennessean*, p. E1.

Quinney, R. (1974). *Critique of legal order: Crime control in capitalist society.* Boston: Little, Brown.

———. (1977). *Class, state, and crime: On the theory and practice of criminal justice.* New York: David McKay.

RAND. (1997). *Mandatory minimum drug sentences: Throwing away the key or the taxpayers' money?* Los Angeles: Drug Policy Research Center.

Randall, W. S. (1993). *Thomas Jefferson: A life.* New York: Harper Perennial.

Reeves, R. (1993). *President Kennedy: Profile of power.* New York: Touchstone Books.

Reich, R. (2002). *I'll be short: Essentials for a decent working society.* Boston: Beacon Press.

Reiman, J. (2004 [1979]). *The rich get richer and the poor get prison: Ideology, class, and criminal justice.* New York: Allyn and Bacon.

Robbins, I. (1998, September 30). Statement before the Joint Senate-House Judiciary Committee of the Oregon Legislature.

Roosevelt, M. (2004). Bizarre, draconian, and disproportionate? In *Time Magazine Special Edition on Criminal Justice* (pp. 38–39). Upper Saddle River, N.J.: Pearson/Prentice-Hall.

Rose, D., & T. Clear. (1998). Incarceration, social capital, and crime: Implications for social disorganization theory. *Criminology, 36*(3), 441–79.

Rouse, T., & P. Unnithan. (1993). Comparative ideologies and alcoholism: The Protestant ethic and proletarian ethics. *Social Problems, 40*(2), 213–27.

Rumsbarger, J. J. (1989). *Profits, power, and Prohibition: Alcohol reform and the industrializing of America, 1800–1930.* New York: SUNY Press.

Rusche, G., & O. Kirchheimer. (1968 [1939]). *Punishment and social structure.* New York: Russell and Russell.

Ryan, M. (1989). *Privatization and the penal system: The American experience and the debate in Britain.* New York: St. Martin's Press.

Ryan, M., & T. Ward. (1989). Managing private prisons. *Howard Journal of Criminal Justice, 28*(3).

Sabol, W. (2002). A national look at prisoner reentry. Paper presented at the Academy of Criminal Justice Sciences Meetings, Washington, D.C.

Sampson, R. J., & S. W. Raudenbush. (2001, February). *Disorder in urban neighborhoods—does it lead to crime?* National Institute of Justice Research Brief. Washington, D.C.: National Institute of Justice.

Sampson, R. J., & W. J. Wilson. (2000). Toward a theory of race, crime, and urban inequality. In R. Crutchfield, G. Bridges, J. Weis, & C. Kubrin (Eds.), *Crime: Readings* (2nd ed.) (pp. 126–37). Thousand Oaks, Calif.: Pine Forge Press.

Sangiacomo, M. (2001, April 25). Prison's closing seen as disaster for Youngstown. *Cleveland Plain Dealer,* p. B7.

Scheingold, S. A. (1991). *The politics of street crime: Criminal process and cultural obsession.* Philadelphia: Temple University Press.

Schlosser, E. (1998). The prison industrial complex. *Atlantic Monthly, 282*(6), 51–77.

Schwartz, M. D., & D. O. Friedrichs. (1994). Postmodern thought and criminological discontent: New metaphors for understanding violence. *Criminology,* 32(2), 221–46.

Seigel, L. (2001). *Criminology* (7th ed.). Belmont, Calif.: Wadsworth.

Sellin, T. (1938). *Culture conflict and crime.* New York: Social Science Research Council.

———. (1976). *Slavery and the penal system.* New York: Elsevier.

Sewell, W. H. (1992). A theory of structure: Duality, agency, and transformation. *American Journal of Sociology, 98,* 1–29.

Shaw, C., & H. D. McKay. (1969). *Juvenile delinquency and urban areas.* Chicago: University of Chicago Press.

Shelden, R. (2001). *Controlling the dangerous classes: A critical introduction to the history of criminal justice.* Boston: Allyn and Bacon.

Sher, A. (1997, April 29). Talks on prison privatization go behind closed hotel doors. *Nashville Banner,* p. A1.

Sherman, M. (1983). Prisons in the theater of American justice. In K. Feinberg (Ed.), *Violent crime in America.* Washington, D.C.: National Policy Exchange.

Sherrill, R. (1984). *Why they call it politics: A guide to America's government* (4th ed.). New York: Harcourt Brace Jovanovich.

Shichor, D. (1995). *Punishment for profit: Private prisons/public concerns.* London: Sage Publications.

———. (1998). Private prisons in perspective: Some conceptual issues. *Howard Journal, 37*(1), 83–100.

Shorris, E. (1997). *New American blues: A journey through poverty to democracy.* New York: W. W. Norton.

Silberman, M. (1995). *A world of violence: Corrections in America.* Boston: Wadsworth.

Simon, J. (1993). *Poor discipline: Parole and the social control of the underclass, 1890–1990.* Chicago: University of Chicago Press.

Simpson, S. S. (Ed.). (2000). *Of crime & criminality: The use of theory in everyday life.* Boston: Pine Forge Press.

Skolnick, J. (1966). *Justice without trial: Law enforcement in a democratic society.* New York: Wiley.

Smith, A. E. (1965). *Colonists in bondage: White servitude and convict labor in America, 1607–1776.* Chapel Hill: University of North Carolina Press.

Smith, R., & R. Cole. (2002, July 17). After four years of legal wrangling, a settlement of the CCA tax lawsuit may be in sight. *Youngstown (Ohio) Vindicator.* Available online at http://www.vindy.com/local_news/275457623695650.shtml.

Sparks, J. R. (2000). Risk and blame in criminal justice controversies. In M. Brown and J. Pratt (Eds.), *Dangerous offenders: Criminal justice and social order* (pp. 127–44). London: Routledge.

Steiner, B. D., W. Bowers, & A. Sarat. (1999). Folk knowledge as legal action: Death penalty judgements and the tenet of early release in a culture of mistrust and punitiveness. *Law & Society Review, 33,* 461–505.

Stoltz, B. A. (1997). Privatizing corrections: Changing the corrections policy-making subgovernment. *Prison Journal, 77*(1), 92–102.

Sullivan, L. (1990). *The prison reform movement: Forlorn hope.* Boston: Twayne.

Surette, R. (1998). *Media, crime, and criminal justice: Images and realities.* Boston: Wadsworth.

Sykes, G. (1974). The rise of critical criminology. *Journal of Criminal Law and Criminology, 65,* 211.

Talvi, S. (2003, January 15). It takes a nation of detention facilities to hold us back: Moral panic and the disaster mentality of immigration policy; an interview with Michael Welch. *Lipmagazine.* Available online at http://www.lipmagazine.org/articles/feattalvi)197_p.htm.

Taylor, R. (1997). Social order and disorder of street blocks and neighborhoods: Ecology, microecology, and the systemic model of social disorganization. *Journal of Research in Crime and Delinquency, 34,* 113–55.

Tennessee Select Oversight Committee on Corrections. (1995, February). *Comparative evaluation of privately managed Corrections Corporation of America prison (South Central Correctional Center) and state-managed prototypical prisons (Northeast Correctional Center, Northwest Correctional Center).* Nashville: Tennessee Select Oversight Committee on Corrections.

Thomas, C. (1995). *Correctional privatization: The issues and the evidence.* Toronto: Fraser Institute.

———. (1996). *Testimony regarding correctional privatization.* Washington, D.C.: Subcommittee on Crime, House Committee on the Judiciary.

TNDOC [Tennessee Department of Corrections]. (1998). *Fiscal year 1998–99 annual report.* Nashville: Tennessee Department of Corrections.

Tonry, M. (1995). *Malign neglect: Race, crime, and punishment in America.* New York: Oxford University Press.

Tonry, M., & J. Petersilia. (2000). *Prisons research at the beginning of the 21st century.* Washington, D.C.: National Institute of Justice.

Touche Ross & Co. (1987). *Privatization in America: An opinion survey of city governments on their use of privatization and their infrastructure needs.* New York: Touche Ross.

Travis, J., A. Solomon, & M. Waul. (2001). *From prison to home: The dimensions and consequences of prisoner reentry.* Washington, D.C.: Urban Institute.

Turk, A. T. (1995). Transformation versus revolutionism and reformism: Policy implications of conflict theory. In H. Barlow (Ed.), *Crime and public policy: Putting theory to work* (pp. 15–28). Boulder: Westview Press.

U.S. Chamber of Commerce. (2005, June 20). Federal prison industries reform. http://www.uschamber.com/issues/index/privatization/fpi.htm.

U.S. expanding prisons to detain more immigrants. (2003, December 7). *Denver Post,* p. A3.

U.S. General Accounting Office. (1996). *Private and public prisons: Studies com-*

paring operational cost and the quality of services. Report to Subcommittee on Crime, Committee on Judiciary, House of Representatives. Washington, D.C.: U.S. General Accounting Office.

Vold, G. B., T. J. Bernard, & J. Snipes. (1998). *Theoretical criminology* (4th ed.). London: Oxford University Press.

Wacquant, L. (1999). "Suitable enemies": Foreigners and immigrants in the prisons of Europe. *Punishment & Society, 1*(2), 215–22.

———. (2001). Deadly symbiosis: When ghetto and prison meet and mesh. In D. Garland (Ed.), *Mass imprisonment: Social causes and consequences* (pp. 82–119). Thousand Oaks, Calif.: Sage.

Wade, P. (1997a, April 20). Insider job? Secrecy clouds prison privatization. *Memphis Commercial Appeal,* p. A6.

———. (1997b, April 30). Senators attend prison-bill briefing closed to public. *Memphis Commercial Appeal,* p. A1.

———. (1997c, May 17). Kyle tries to soothe privatizing skeptics: Foes fear prison concept detrimental to safety, society. *Memphis Commercial Appeal,* p. B1.

———. (1997d, October 24). Lawmakers uneasy on provision for prisons. *Memphis Commercial Appeal,* p. B1.

———. (1997e, November 6). Sundquist hits wall in prison power try: Lawmakers seek voice in privatization move. *Memphis Commercial Appeal,* p. B1.

———. (1998a, September 2). Bill to privatize prisons falls on hard times. *Memphis Commercial Appeal,* p. B1.

———. (1998b, September 24). Sundquist slows privatized prison rush. *Memphis Commercial Appeal,* p. B1.

Walker, A. (1982). *The color purple.* New York: Washington Square Press, Pocket Books.

Walzer, M. (1991). Private prisons are unjust. In R. Espejo (Ed.), *America's prisons: Opposing viewpoints* (pp. 116–17). San Diego: Greenhaven Press.

Welch, M. (1996). The immigration crisis: Detention as an emerging mechanism of social control. *Social Justice: A Journal of Crime, Conflict, & World Order, 23*(3), 169–84.

———. (1999). Social movements and political protest: Exploring flag desecration in the 1960s, 1970s, 1980s. *Social Pathology, 5*(2), 167–86.

———. (2002). *Detained: Immigration laws and the expanding I.N.S. jail complex.* Philadelphia: Temple University Press.

———. (2005 forthcoming). Immigration lockdown before and after 9/11: Ethnic constructions and their consequences. In M. Bosworth and S. Bush-Baskette (Eds.), *Race, gender, and punishment: Theorizing differences.* Boston: Northeastern University Press.

West, C. (1993). *Race matters.* Boston: Beacon Press.

———. (1997). Afterword to W. Lubiano (Ed.), *The house that race built: Black Americans, U.S. terrain* (pp. 301–3). New York: Pantheon Books.

———. (1998). The role of law in progressive politics. In D. Kairys (Ed.), *The politics of law: A progressive critique* (pp. 708–17). Boston: Basic Books.

————. (1999). *The Cornel West reader.* New York: Basic Books.

West, P. (1998a, January 17). Prison bill highlights. *Memphis Commercial Appeal,* p. A1.

————. (1998b, April 1). Plan to privatize prisons faces tough time in senate. *Memphis Commercial Appeal,* p. A7.

Western, B., & K. Beckett. (1999). How unregulated is the U.S. labor market? The penal system as a labor market institution. *American Journal of Sociology, 104*(4), 1030–53.

White, M. D., & M. A. Hallett. (2005 forthcoming). Revisiting anomalous outcome data from the "Breaking the Cycle" program in Jacksonville, Florida. *Journal of Offender Rehabilitation.*

White House Printing Office. (2001). *Unlevel playing field: Barriers to participation by faith-based and community organizations in federal social service programs.* Washington, D.C.: White House Printing Office.

Williams, L. A. (1998). Welfare and entitlements: The social roots of poverty. In D. Kairys (Ed.), *The politics of law: A progressive critique* (pp. 569–89). Boston: Basic Books.

Williams, P. J. (1991). *The alchemy of race and rights.* Cambridge: Harvard University Press.

————. (1995). Alchemical notes: Reconstructing ideals from deconstructed rights. In R. Delgado (Ed.), *Critical race theory: The cutting edge* (pp. 80–90). Philadelphia: Temple University Press.

Wilson, J. Q., & R. Herrnstein. (1985). *Crime & human nature: The definitive study of the causes of crime.* New York: Simon and Schuster.

Wilson, W. J. (1996). *When work disappears: The world of the new urban poor.* New York: Alfred A. Knopf.

————. (1999). *The bridge over the racial divide: Rising inequality and coalition politics.* Berkeley and Los Angeles: University of California Press.

Wittenberg, P. M. (1996). Power, influence, and the development of correctional policy. *Federal Probation, 60*(2), 43–48.

Woodward, B. (1996). *The Choice.* New York: Simon and Schuster.

Yngvesson, B. (1997). Negotiating motherhood: Identity and difference in "open" adoptions. *Law & Society Review, 31*(1), 31–80.

Zald, M. (1964). Review of *Symbolic crusade: Politics and the American temperance movement,* by J. Gusfield. *American Journal of Sociology, 70*(3), 392–93.

Zimring, F., & G. F. Hawkins. (1997). *Crime is not the problem: Lethal violence in America.* New York: Oxford University Press.

Zinn, H. (1980). *A people's history of the United States.* New York: Harper and Row.

INDEX

The numbers in italics refer to figures or tables.

MICHAEL HALLETT, PH.D., is Associate Professor of Criminal Justice at the University of North Florida, where he is also Chair of the Department of Criminology and Criminal Justice. He is also Director of the Center for Race and Juvenile Justice Policy.

RANDALL G. SHELDEN is Professor of Criminal Justice at the University of Nevada at Las Vegas and the author and coauthor of several books and articles on crime and criminal justice, most recently *Controlling the Dangerous Classes: A Critical Introduction to the History of Criminal Justice* and *Criminal Justice in America: A Critical View* (both published by Allyn and Bacon).

Critical Perspectives in Criminology

Philosophy, Crime, and Criminology
  Edited by Bruce A. Arrigo and
  Christopher R. Williams
Private Prisons in America: A Critical
  Race Perspective   *Michael A. Hallett*

The University of Illinois Press
is a founding member of the
Association of American University Presses.

———————————————————————

Composed in 9.5/13 Trump Mediaeval
with Meta display
by Jim Proefrock
at the University of Illinois Press
Designed by Paula Newcomb
Manufactured by Cushing-Malloy, Inc.

University of Illinois Press
1325 South Oak Street
Champaign, IL 61820-6903
www.press.uillinois.edu